matt dawson

fresh. simple. tasty.

matt dawson

fresh. simple. tasty.

NEW HOLLAND

Published in 2009 by New Holland Publishers (UK) Ltd
London • Cape Town • Sydney • Auckland
www.newhollandpublishers.com

Garfield House
86–88 Edgware Road
London W2 2EA
United Kingdom

80 McKenzie Street
Cape Town 8001
South Africa

Unit 1
66 Gibbes Street
Chatswood
NSW 2067
Australia

218 Lake Road
Northcote
Auckland
New Zealand

ISBN   978 1 84773 586 7

Senior Editor   Corinne Masciocchi
Development Editor   Jane Bamforth
Design Concept   e-Digital Design
Mac Artworker   Peter Gwyer
Photographic Art Direction and Jacket Design   Simon Daley
Photography   Tony Briscoe
Food Styling   Clare Greenstreet
Production   Laurence Poos
Editorial Direction   Rosemary Wilkinson

1 3 5 7 9 10 8 6 4 2

Reproduction by Pica Digital PTE Ltd, Singapore
Printed and bound by Tien Wah Press PTE Ltd, Singapore

Disclaimer
The author and publishers have made every effort to ensure that all information given in this book is safe and accurate, but they cannot accept liability for any resulting injury or loss or damage to either property or person, whether direct or consequential or however arising.

contents

foreword

Back in 2003 I was working in the kitchen at Nobu London when a waiter told me that Matt Dawson was in the restaurant having dinner. It was just after the rugby World Cup, where England had made that glorious victory and they were now World Champions. Being a huge rugby fan and in awe of that final pass Matt produced, I told the waiter 'Please tell Mr Dawson that dinner is on the Chef'. It's the least I could do for making me such a happy and proud Englishman – and a slightly richer one for winning a bet with a fellow Australian chef!

You would think that professional rugby players' staple diet consists of 'meat and two veg' but I was surprised to learn that this was not the case. Matt has become a regular diner at Nobu, and we always try out our new dishes on him to gain his much welcome feedback and you could say that he has now become the Nobu tasting guinea pig. Matt has also brought in to Nobu large tables of fellow rugby players, and to my surprise, they all relish the food and flavours, albeit ordering rather larger quantities than our regular diners!

Ever since our first meeting I have discovered Matt's keen interest in food and cooking, and we have become firm friends. Matt has spent some time working with me in Nobu so he could learn more about what we do in the kitchens and I can only say that I wish I had a kitchen full of Dawsons. He applies the same unfaltering determination and will to succeed in the kitchen as he does on the rugby pitch and will not stop until he achieves perfection.

Matt has developed his own style of cooking from all types of cuisine and one thing for sure is that his dishes and recipes are not only delicious masterpieces but also modern and healthy in their composition. His recipes are ones that can be used with ease at home for both casual eating or dinner parties.

This book is a fine collection of his new-found passion and he has brought together a brilliant nexus of culinary delights. I would encourage all admirers and followers of fine food to 'devour' this book with all five senses.

Mark Edwards
Executive Chef, Nobu

introduction

I'm sitting in Orlando airport at a sushi bar called 'One Flew South'. It appealed to me because of its minimalistic decor and amazing display of fresh fish. That, of course, coupled with the two Japanese chefs on show chopping and rolling at breakneck speed. A quick glance at the menu and I was sold, despite the fairly hefty price by each dish – a turn-off for some, but when it comes to food I'm a sucker for quality and don't mind paying a little extra. I'm not frivolous with my money but having been involved in a few restaurants, either through friends or work, I never complain about the price. Naturally, it better be good!

Anyway, back to why I was telling you this. I feel like I'm back at school, leaving my homework until the last minute, except in this case my editor is chasing me for this intro. So here goes... under the inspiration of a Californian roll and three slices of very expensive yellow-tail sashimi.

Well, I should start with why I dramatically changed tack from being a professional rugby player to a general foodie and aspiring cook. First and foremost my health is paramount; without it all else is irrelevant, so I try to do whatever I can to adhere to a healthy lifestyle. Of course, with so many temptations around it's hard to go through life being good all the time, and to be honest a little indulgence isn't always a bad thing. I just never see the need to consume unnecessary 'rubbish' without good reason. Does it taste good? How often am I doing it? When am I eating it? What does my body get out of it? With so many possible flavour combinations even the most boring salad can be transformed into a mouth-watering delight.

Besides general good health, I had to ensure I was providing fuel for my body when I was playing professional rugby. If I wanted to aspire to international standards, my diet had to change dramatically: a balanced, healthy diet was therefore on the cards. Eating the right foods at the right times can have amazing effects on both your mental and physical wellbeing. But how many of you keen foodies skip breakfast because of the morning rush? Whether it's because you're late for the school run or just too tired from the night before, don't dart out the front door without a good, wholesome breakfast inside you. Heading out for the day on an empty stomach just won't set you up to a good start. I'm hoping to change people's morning routines by suggesting they get up 15 minutes earlier to prepare a simple, flavoursome breakfast, which will ignite their body and mind so that the rest of the day is more productive. Give it a go and come and find me if after a couple of months you don't feel more alert and less hungry during the day. After all, as the saying goes: eat breakfast like a king, lunch like a prince and dinner like a pauper.

I think I have always had a little talent in the kitchen. At the tender age of 14, I embarked on my first job at the George & Dragon in Marlow. Unfortunately I wasn't working in the actual restaurant but behind the swing doors, scraping food off plates, draining half-eaten knickerbocker glories and washing the dirty dishes. Oh yes, I became a dab hand at mopping floors too! However, experiencing first hand the inner workings of a restaurant intrigued me, and the co-ordination from order to service still amazes me.

I left it a mere 20 years before I revisited a restaurant kitchen. It was for Celebrity MasterChef in 2006. I had just retired from London Wasps and England, and in all honestly my next professional move wasn't fully firmed up. My management company put me forward as they knew I could regularly be found dining in the West End of London, but little did they know my competitive spirit would transfer so seamlessly from the oval ball to the oven.

Here steps in my mentor, Mr Mark Edwards, the least likely looking Worldwide Executive Chef of Nobu. A short, rotund, bald-headed London geezer… who, it is safe to say, is a culinary genius. We met in Nobu London after the rugby World Cup in Australia during 2003 and have been friends ever since. A perfect match as I love food and he loves rugby. In passing, I mentioned I was having a go at this MasterChef thing. His response was brief and to the point: 'Right, let's win it!'. He had me in the kitchen at Nobu Berkeley every day for a month, teaching me not only the intricacies of Japanese food preparation, but more traditional styles of cooking too, such as Italian, French and English. We'd design new dishes (which are included in this book) and he'd continually test my palate as well as my technical skills, which turned my newfound hobby into something of an obsession.

I hope that by reading this cookbook and trying out some of the recipes yourself you'll see that by getting to grips with the finer points of cookery (herbs, spices, seasoning and presentation), you can transform a regular dish into a real crowd pleaser. It really is that easy. How many TV cookery shows have you watched where the chef throws a few bits together and, hey presto, the crowd goes wild? Guys, it is so doable it's scary! Just spend a bit of time stocking the larder with some essentials and buy as much fresh produce as you can: food markets, fishmongers and local butchers are all ideal but don't shy away from supermarkets or even frozen foods. The demand we place on being able to purchase all manner of ingredients all year round means the frozen foods market is crucial and continues to offer the consumer more and more choice.

What makes my cookbook special over the hundreds of others on offer? Well, I don't profess to be a master chef by any stretch of the imagination but what I am is realistic. Take my schedule. I can't remember the last time I had two weeks the same. One day I may play golf in the morning then host a radio show at 9 pm. The next day I might not wake up until 10 am (I have no children before you ask!) but be on the road for a corporate event in Sheffield and won't arrive back home until 1 am. The weekends vary from following the England team with Radio 5 Live or lazing about in the garden with friends and a few bottles of wine.

So, how can I practise what I preach by eating well despite my madly irregular schedule? I need to be switched on whatever I'm doing, so planning what and when to eat has now become a habit rather than a chore. The purpose of these recipes is to enable you to find something that will enhance your repertoire, whatever your circumstances. Not only that, but you'll also be ticking all the right boxes: wellness, nutrition, simplicity and of course, taste. Yes, there are some heavier dishes that require a little more time and effort, and perhaps the fat fairy may frown upon them but remember, it's all about balance. A vast majority of the recipes can be rustled up in no time at all and yet the recipient will still be wowed, I guarantee!

As I dunk my sushi in the soy sauce for one final mouthful, I think I've managed to convey why I'm mad about food. To all those people who have had to endure my efforts before the more accomplished third attempt, I apologise. To my mum who is the best cook ever – especially at Christmas when she still makes cooking for the eight of us look like a stroll in the park – thanks for the inspiration! There is also a blond-haired pretty boy called Brett Taylor who has to take enormous credit for setting me on the right path. When I first played professional rugby we lived together and he ruled the roost – in the kitchen at least. Thankfully he passed on his 'salmon in a bag' recipe, which I now plagiarise. Sorry pal! Mind you, I do remember him leaving a stewed rabbit in the Aga for three days until the rancid smell emanating from the house had the neighbourhood up in arms!

I hope this is just the start of my culinary experience. Not for one moment did I think I'd be writing my own book or travelling the length and breadth of the British coastline filming a food show with restaurateur Mitch Tonks. What on earth will the next chapter be? Well, with any luck it will involve eating, drinking and then some more eating and drinking. Enjoy!

breakfast

scrambled eggs
on soda bread toast with marmite

You must think I'm mad... We all know you either love Marmite or hate it. Needless to say, I love it! I don't slather it on, I use just enough to taste. During the Lions Tour of 1997 I decided to give this simple recipe a go. We won the game that day so naturally it was down to my choice of breakfast. That trip lasted nine weeks and we won the series 2–1. I probably consumed a whole jar of the stuff in that time, so an eternal thanks to Marmite for the victory!

SODA BREAD	PREPARATION TIME 15 MINUTES	COOKING TIME 30–35 MINUTES
EGGS	PREPARATION TIME 2 MINUTES	COOKING TIME 5 MINUTES

FOR THE SODA BREAD (MAKES 20-CM LOAF)

Butter, for greasing
Plain flour, for dusting
400 g wholemeal flour
30 g butter, cubed
2 tsp bicarbonate of soda
40 g soft brown sugar
½ tsp salt
220 ml buttermilk

FOR THE SCRAMBLED EGGS (SERVES 2)

Knob of butter
4 free-range eggs, beaten
Freshly-ground black pepper
Butter and Marmite, to serve

1 Start by making the bread. Preheat the oven to 220°C/425°F (gas mark 7). Grease a 20-cm square, 5-cm deep non-stick tin and dust it with plain flour. Grease a 30-cm square of foil.

2 Place the flour in a large mixing bowl and rub the butter in using your fingertips. Stir in the bicarbonate of soda, brown sugar and salt.

3 Mix the buttermilk in a jug with 220 ml cold water. Gradually pour the liquid into the dry ingredients and stir well using a table knife. Transfer the mixture to the prepared tin and smooth down the surface with the back of a wet metal spoon.

4 Cover the dough with lightly greased foil and press it down on the surface so that it will stay in place during cooking. Bake in the oven for 20 minutes. Remove the foil and reduce the oven temperature to 200°C/400°F (gas mark 6). Bake for a further 10 to 15 minutes, or until the loaf is just starting to brown. Allow the loaf to cool in the tin for 10 minutes, then remove and cool on a wire rack.

5 While the bread is cooling, prepare the eggs. Melt the butter in a small non-stick pan over a medium heat. Pour in the eggs, cook over a gentle heat for 3 to 5 minutes, stirring constantly with a wooden spoon, until just beginning to scramble.

6 Toast four slices of the soda bread and spread with butter and Marmite. Divide the egg between two plates and season well with pepper. Serve with the toast and Marmite.

winter breakfast

Many mornings in the coldest and darkest of winters I'd peel myself out of bed, draw back the curtains and wish I'd chosen another profession! An office worker, banker, chef or even a driving instructor would have been much more appealing than rolling around in freezing mud and ice baths. Of course, the grass is always greener and yes, I jest! You've got be warm on the inside and the slow-release energy in porridge, coupled with a mug of hot chocolate, couldn't be a more perfect start to a busy, active day.

SERVES 1   **PREPARATION TIME** 7 MINUTES   **COOKING TIME** 4½ MINUTES

FOR THE PORRIDGE

50 g porridge oats
200 ml soya milk
1–2 tsp clear honey
1 Tbsp chopped hazelnuts

FOR THE HOT CHOCOLATE

250 ml soya milk
1 tsp cocoa powder
1–2 tsp clear honey

1 Start by making the porridge. Place the oats and soya milk in a large heatproof cereal bowl. Cook in the microwave for 2½ minutes on full power.

2 In the meantime, prepare the hot chocolate. Pour the milk into a mug and heat in the microwave on full power for 2 minutes. Sprinkle the cocoa powder over the milk and stir well. Add honey to taste.

3 Remove the porridge from the microwave, stir well, add honey to taste, sprinkle over the chopped hazelnuts, and serve immediately.

A cheeky hot chocolate in the morning always goes down well...

poached eggs and ham

In a time of health-conscious eating, some real favourites seem to be getting the cold shoulder. Bacon and eggs were, and still are, part of my staple diet, but I've adapted this firm favourite a little. No, I don't fry the bacon in lard and slap a load of butter on the bread but I can still indulge myself with some slight amendments. Don't forget the brown sauce... perfect!

SERVES 1   PREPARATION TIME 10 MINUTES   COOKING TIME 3 MINUTES

4 slices of Parma ham

Drop of white wine vinegar

2 free-range eggs

Buttered toast and brown sauce, to serve

1 Preheat the grill to medium and lay the Parma ham on a baking sheet.

2 In a small pan, bring 3 cm (1 1/4 in) of water to a gentle simmer with a drop of vinegar. Break the first egg into a small bowl or cup and then very carefully add it to the pan. Repeat immediately with the second egg. Cook the eggs for 3 minutes each, spooning water over occasionally.

3 Meanwhile, place the ham under the preheated grill and cook for 2 minutes, or until crispy.

4 Use a slotted spoon to remove the first egg that went in and then the second egg. Drain on absorbent kitchen paper to remove any excess water. Serve the ham and eggs on hot buttered toast with lashings of brown sauce.

potato brunch omelette

Blimey, I've had some hangovers in my time and it doesn't get any easier now the years are adding up! But we all need to get together every so often and what better occasion to do this than the 6 Nations. I usually have a few mates over to watch the match, or we go to my local for a few beers, then we all crash out at mine. And what better way to settle the stomach and share the evening's stories over a hearty omelette. The bacon bits really give this simple dish lots of flavour.

SERVES 2   PREPARATION TIME 20 MINUTES   COOKING TIME 10 MINUTES

1 Heat the oil in a 30-cm non-stick frying pan. Add the onion and cook over a medium heat for 5 minutes, stirring occasionally. Add the bacon pieces, stir well and cook for a couple of minutes.

2 Add the tomatoes and potatoes to the pan, and cook for 5 minutes, stirring occasionally.

3 Season the beaten eggs and pour into the pan. Swirl so that the egg covers the whole base of the pan. Cook the omelette for 5 minutes, or until the egg is set underneath. Meanwhile, preheat the grill to high.

4 Place the pan under the grill (protect the handle with foil if it isn't heatproof) and grill the omelette for 5 minutes, or until the egg on the top is cooked. Remove the pan carefully from the grill, cut the omelette into quarters and divide between two plates. Serve with buttered toast and ketchup.

1 Tbsp olive oil
1 onion, peeled and finely sliced
4 rashers back bacon, chopped into bite-size pieces
10 cherry tomatoes, halved
175–200 g boiled potatoes, peeled and roughly cubed
4 eggs, beaten
Salt and freshly-ground black pepper
Buttered toast and tomato ketchup, to serve

breakfast pancakes
with fresh fruit and maple syrup

I can't start the day without breakfast. It sounds silly but sometimes I wake up excited just thinking about what I can rustle up to kick-start my day. Actually, it's very important to eat a proper breakfast. I tend to enjoy working out in the morning or even playing golf on a full stomach. Of course you can have bacon sandwiches and eggs on toast but balance it with some of these beauties!

MAKES 6 MEDIUM PANCAKES   PREPARATION TIME 10 MINUTES   COOKING TIME 30 MINUTES

1 Sieve the flour into a large mixing bowl. Add the eggs, one at a time, and stir well with a fork, until incorporated.

2 Gradually add the milk, stirring well after each addition. Slowly add 100 ml water to the batter and whisk well with an electric whisk or fork until the mixture is smooth. Pour the batter into a large jug.

3 Heat a knob of butter in a 20-cm diameter non-stick frying pan. Once the butter has melted, swirl it around the pan and then pour it away.

4 Pour in enough of the pancake batter to thinly coat the base of the pan, swirling it a little to distribute it evenly. Cook the pancake for 1 to 2 minutes until just starting to turn golden on the underside. Using a metal palette knife, flip the pancake over and cook the other side until golden.

5 Slide the cooked pancake onto a plate and serve immediately with your choice of fruit and maple syrup. Meanwhile, repeat the process to use up all the batter, coating the pan with butter and pouring it off after every three pancakes.

100 g plain flour
2 medium free-range eggs
180 ml semi-skimmed milk
Butter, for cooking
Fresh fruit of your choice (I like strawberries, blueberries and pineapple) and maple syrup, to serve

summer breakfast

How many times, like me, have you stumbled down the stairs still blurry eyed from your deep sleep wondering what you'll have for breakfast? By the time you get to the fridge you're probably excited by a healthy bowl of muesli to set you up for the day. But then you realise there's no milk or it's gone off. Don't ask me why, but one morning I threw the rest of a carton of apple juice in and it worked a treat. As for the smoothie, never mind your five-a-day – you can tick off most of your daily dose in one hit here. And besides, when you're used to having to down pints of whey protein (which tastes like dust by the way) after a weights session, smoothies are like sweet nectar. The more berries the better!

SERVES 2   PREPARATION TIME 20 MINUTES PLUS OVERNIGHT SOAKING

FOR THE MUESLI

4 Tbsp rolled oats
6 Tbsp apple juice
3 Tbsp mixed dried fruit (e.g. raisins, apricots, pineapple, mango, pear, cranberries, banana chips), finely chopped
½ Tbsp roughly-chopped hazelnuts
½ Tbsp flaked almonds
Soya milk or 0% fat Greek or plain low-fat yoghurt, to serve

FOR THE SMOOTHIE

1 banana, peeled and sliced
10 strawberries, hulled
3 Tbsp blueberries
1 egg white
2 Tbsp plain low-fat yoghurt
Chilled cranberry or apple juice, to serve

1 To make the muesli, place the oats and apple juice in a medium bowl, stir well, cover and leave at room temperature to soak overnight.

2 In the morning, add the remaining ingredients to the bowl and stir well. Serve with soya milk or yoghurt.

3 To make the smoothie, place the banana, strawberries, blueberries, egg white and yoghurt in a blender or food processor and whiz until smooth.

4 Pour the smoothie into two tall glasses and top up with cranberry or apple juice. Stir well and serve straight away.

breakfast muffins

It's not always easy to find food that doesn't have a little naughtiness in it. Sometimes it's the crackling on a pork roast you just can't resist or maybe the eternal quandary of what to buy at the petrol station: crisps, chocolate and fizzy drinks all fill me with guilt but what are the other options? Homemade muffins of course! The lesser of two evils it's true, but hopefully nibbling on one of these delicious creations while you pound the tarmac of the M25 will provide reason to follow this recipe and make the finest muffins. By the way, the kitchen will smell amazing for the rest of the day.

MAKES 18   PREPARATION TIME 20 MINUTES   COOKING TIME 20–25 MINUTES

1 Preheat the oven to 200°C/400°F (gas mark 6) and place 18 paper muffin cases on a baking tray.

2 Sift the flour, baking powder and cinnamon into a bowl and stir in the sugar. In a large jug, combine the milk, eggs and melted butter, and beat well.

3 Pour the wet ingredients into the centre of the dry ingredients and mix well. Add the fruit of your choice and combine quickly. The mixture will be quite runny and lumpy. Spoon the mixture into the muffin cases. Bake for 20 to 25 minutes until well risen and pale golden on top.

4 Serve warm or allow to cool on a wire rack and store in an airtight container for a couple of days. Alternatively, allow the muffins to cool then place in a plastic box with a lid and freeze.

TIP

These muffins freeze well – I like to have a supply of them in the freezer and take out as many as I need. They only take an hour or so to thaw out and can then be warmed through in the oven for 5 minutes at 180°C/350°F (gas mark 4).

350 g plain white flour

1 Tbsp baking powder

1 tsp ground cinnamon

175 g light muscovado sugar

150 ml semi-skimmed milk

3 large free-range eggs

150 g butter, melted

FOR BANANA AND APRICOT MUFFINS, ADD

2 bananas, mashed
2 Tbsp finely-chopped ready-to-eat dried apricots

FOR APPLE AND RAISIN MUFFINS, ADD

2 dessert apples, peeled, cored and grated
2 Tbsp raisins

kiwi toast

New Zealanders always do things just that little bit differently. Yes, yes – they're good at, if not obsessed with rugby, but their culinary reputation has some way to go to catch up with the All Blacks. Perhaps a bit harsh though as Mudbrick Island, just off Auckland Harbour, gave myself and the BBC 5 Live team some great evenings whilst we were over there covering the 2008 summer tour. Back at the Auckland Hilton, however, it was a bog standard buffet breakfast pretty much everyday, with the only highlight being their interpretation of eggy bread. Fair play – another great export alongside Sir Edmund Hillary.

SERVES 2   PREPARATION TIME 10 MINUTES   COOKING TIME 2–4 MINUTES

3 eggs
½ tsp ground cinnamon
2 Tbsp caster sugar
4 slices of white or fruit bread
15 g butter
Sieved icing sugar, to serve

1 Place the eggs, cinnamon and caster sugar in a shallow bowl and whisk until frothy.

2 Dip the bread into the egg mixture and turn the slices a couple of times to make sure they are thoroughly coated.

3 Melt the butter in a large frying pan over a medium heat. Fry the slices of egg-coated bread for 1 minute on each side, or until the egg has set and is starting to turn golden brown.

4 Cut the slices of toast in half and place on two plates. Sprinkle with sieved icing sugar and serve hot.

my favourite cereal
and fruit combos

This page will make breakfast time so much more enjoyable. If you're like me and have all of three minutes to think about what to scoff in the morning before rushing off to work, then these quick and simple suggestions will make your life so much easier. All you need is a selection of fresh and dried fruit. The beauty of these ideas is that there is always a flavoursome choice available, no matter how late you get up. And remember, a breakfast of a king will set you up for the day!

FRESH FRUIT IDEAS

Cornflakes with chopped peach or nectarine

Shreddies with chopped pear

Bran Flakes with halved red and green grapes

Porridge with grated apple

Shredded Wheat with strawberries, bananas and apples

Rice Krispies with raspberries

Muesli with blueberries

DRIED FRUIT IDEAS

Shredded Wheat with dried cranberries

Cornflakes with banana chips

Shreddies with chopped dried melon

Bran Flakes with chopped dried apricots

Porridge with chopped dried pear, raisins and dessicated coconut

Rice Krispies with chopped dried pineapple

starters

citrus chilli scallops

Whilst filming Mitch and Matt's Big Fish with Mitch Tonks, we visited the sleepy town of Tarbet in Scotland. Though not renowned for its nightlife, we did manage to consume a fair few glasses of Scotch. Very nice too. What we did have access to was the bounty of Loch Fyne. The scallops were the size of side plates, with flesh to match. Seeing them caught by hand and lovingly brought ashore demonstrated that some foods need little addition – just season and eat as nature intended.

SERVES 4   PREPARATION TIME 10 MINUTES   COOKING TIME 2 MINUTES

½ cucumber, seeded and sliced into
    fine 6–8 cm strips

1 small red chilli, pounded in a pestle and mortar

Zest and juice of 1 lime

Zest and juice of 1 orange

1 Tbsp olive oil

8 roeless scallops

Fresh coriander leaves, to garnish

1 Arrange the cucumber strips on four plates. In a small jug, combine the chilli, lime and orange zests and juices.

2 In a medium non-stick frying pan heat the oil over a high heat and fry the scallops for 1 minute on each side.

3 Divide the scallops between the plates and garnish with a coriander leaf. Drizzle 1 to 2 teaspoons of the dressing over and serve immediately.

Mitch and me on location in Cromer. When it comes to fish, he's the man.

prawn cocktail

Actually, on reflection, I may have been cooking longer than I thought. When I was a kid, my job on Christmas day was to prepare the prawn cocktail starter for lunch. Not the most enormous task, I agree, yet possibly the most important. Everybody loves prawn cocktail; just make sure the lettuce isn't limp and soggy and don't forget to defrost the prawns (like I did one year). No one commented, so it must have been OK...

SERVES 4   PREPARATION TIME 10 MINUTES

1 To make the dressing, combine the mayonnaise, ketchup and whisky in a medium bowl. Season well and add a dash or two of Tabasco sauce to taste. Stir well.

2 Add the prawns to the dressing. Stir carefully to thoroughly coat the prawns without breaking them up.

3 Divide the lettuce and spring onions between four glasses. Top each with a quarter of the prawn mixture and season well with plenty of freshly-ground black pepper. Serve with brown bread and lemon wedges.

| 2 Tbsp mayonnaise |
| 2 Tbsp tomato ketchup |
| 2 tsp whisky |
| Maldon sea salt and freshly-ground black pepper |
| Tabasco sauce, to taste |
| 175 g shelled frozen prawns, thoroughly defrosted |
| ¼ iceberg lettuce, finely shredded |
| 2 spring onions, finely shredded |
| Thinly-sliced brown bread and butter, and lemon wedges, to serve |

Two of my biggest prawn cocktail fans, nephew Daniel and niece Ellen.

broccoli and stilton soup

Get your stopwatch out and see if you can break my record of 10 minutes to make this tasty starter. No frills or spills, just loads of goodness. By the way, if you don't have stock just use the water you boil the broccoli in, along with plenty of seasoning. You can use a smoothie maker or one of those handheld whizzers is really handy. Remember the technique as it's similar for making all veggie soups: mushrooms, cauliflower, parsnips or pea and ham. Your repertoire has just multiplied tenfold!

SERVES 4   PREPARATION TIME 10 MINUTES   COOKING TIME 10 MINUTES

2 Tbsp olive oil
25 g butter
1 onion, peeled and finely chopped
1 clove of garlic, peeled and finely chopped
500 g broccoli florets and stalks, roughly chopped
750 ml good-quality vegetable stock
150 g Stilton, cubed
Freshly-ground black pepper
2 Tbsp double cream and grated whole nutmeg, to garnish
Crusty wholemeal bread, to serve

1 Heat the olive oil and butter in a large pan, and gently fry the onion and garlic for 4 to 5 minutes, or until softened.

2 Add the broccoli and stock to the pan, bring to the boil, then reduce the heat to medium. Cover and simmer for 5 minutes, or until the broccoli is very tender, stirring occasionally. Whiz the soup in a food processor until smooth.

3 Return the soup to a clean pan, add the Stilton and stir until melted. Season to taste with black pepper and ladle into four bowls. Swirl 1/2 tablespoon of cream in each bowl and top with plenty of grated nutmeg. Serve piping hot with wholemeal bread.

chilli-cheese mushroom melts

It's always handy to have a few vegetarian options available. I find mushrooms a great complement to most flavours. Who doesn't have tomatoes, onions, olive oil, salt, pepper and garlic in the kitchen? These are perfect late-night nibbles if you're worried about eating carbs before bedtime. In fact, that's exactly how I made up this recipe: totally starving after a late night celebrating a win for England! It's not always easy cooking when you're a little bit tipsy but this recipe is ridiculously simple.

SERVES 4   **PREPARATION TIME 10 MINUTES**   **COOKING TIME 10 MINUTES**

8 large portobello mushrooms	
2 Tbsp extra virgin olive oil	
Salt and freshly-ground black pepper	
8 Tbsp salsa	
8 tsp grated Parmesan cheese	

1 Preheat the grill to medium. Brush the mushrooms all over with oil. Place the mushrooms, stalk-side down, on a baking tray and season well. Grill for 2 minutes.

2 Turn the mushrooms over and top each with 1 tablespoon of salsa and grill for 5 minutes. Remove the tray from the heat and sprinkle 1 teaspoon of Parmesan over each mushroom.

3 Return the mushrooms to the grill for a further 3 minutes, or until the cheese is golden and bubbling. Serve immediately.

squid with white beans

Squid is one of the most popular choices of starter at restaurants but we are unlikely to buy fresh squid and replicate the dish at home. Why not? Well, it's not the most attractive of seafood, but your fishmonger could deal with that and prepare the squid rings for you. I love this type of food: clean, fresh, and full of complementary flavours and textures. Don't forget the lime: it brings the dish to life.

SERVES 4   PREPARATION TIME 10 MINUTES   COOKING TIME 15 MINUTES

4 Tbsp extra virgin olive oil

1 red chilli, finely chopped

2 Tbsp white wine vinegar

400-g tin haricot beans, rinsed and drained

Salt and freshly-ground black pepper

100 g beansprouts

50 g shiso cress or rocket leaves

4 Tbsp plain flour

300 g ready-prepared fresh squid rings

3 Tbsp olive oil

2 Tbsp chopped fresh coriander

Lime wedges, to serve

1 Place the extra virgin olive oil in a medium pan with the chilli, white wine vinegar and beans. Season and cook over a low heat to gently warm through.

2 Divide the beansprouts and cress or rocket leaves among four small plates.

3 Place the flour, squid rings and plenty of seasoning in a large food bag and shake well to coat the rings. Remove the squid from the bag and shake off any excess flour.

4 Heat the olive oil to high in a griddle pan and fry the squid in batches for 1 to 2 minutes.

5 Stir the coriander into the bean mixture and divide it among the plates. Top with the squid and serve with lime wedges.

squid tempura
with chilli dipping sauce

Squid is a total weakness of mine, but it always seems to be on the menu in a style which fails to tempt me. I wasn't a fan of squid until I started travelling to the Mediterranean on holiday. The Spanish and Italians are the masters, whether it's in tapas or a salad. Don't even think about overcooking it or you'll hunt me down and question my love affair with it!

SERVES 4   PREPARATION TIME 15 MINUTES   COOKING TIME 15–20 MINUTES

1 Start by making the dipping sauce by mixing together all the ingredients in a small bowl or jar.

2 To make the batter, mix the plain flour, cornflour and baking powder with a pinch of salt in a bowl, and whisk in enough cold water to get a mixture the consistency of double cream.

3 Heat a pan one-third filled with the vegetable oil for deep-frying, until a breadcrumb will sizzle gently in it.

4 Dip a piece of squid into the batter and carefully lower it into the hot fat. Repeat until you have about six pieces cooking at a time. Cook for 2 to 3 minutes, until golden brown and crisp. Remove the squid from the oil with a slotted spoon and drain on kitchen paper. Repeat to use up all the squid. Serve the hot squid with the dipping sauce.

FOR THE CHILLI DIPPING SAUCE

3-cm piece fresh root ginger, very finely chopped
½ tsp sugar
1 Tbsp chopped fresh coriander
½ Tbsp chopped fresh mint
1 red chilli, finely chopped
2 Tbsp soy sauce
2 Tbsp Chinese rice wine or pale dry sherry

FOR THE SQUID

55 g plain flour
55 g cornflour
Pinch of baking powder
Salt
300 g ready-prepared fresh squid rings
Vegetable oil, for deep frying

easy canapés

I should really thank Georgie for letting me sneak this recipe into the book. She is the mother-in-law of my good friend Tim Rodber, who played for Northampton, England and the Lions with me. Tim's a very busy man, but now and again invites me down to Sussex to escape the London chaos. What seals the deal for me is the aroma from Tim's kitchen. It's the type of house that always seems to have something simmering away in the Aga. Last Christmas, these canapés caught my eye and even though I tried my best to seek out the ingredients, Georgie kept them close to her chest! I hope I got the general gist of them in these moreish marvels.

SERVES 4   **PREPARATION TIME** 15 MINUTES   **COOKING TIME** 10 MINUTES

---

150 g cream cheese
2 spring onions, finely chopped
25 g Parmesan cheese, finely grated
Maldon sea salt and freshly-ground black pepper
4 thick slices of white bread
Paprika, to garnish

1 Preheat the oven to 200°C/400°F (gas mark 6).

2 Place the cream cheese, spring onions, Parmesan and plenty of seasoning in a medium bowl, and mash together using a fork.

3 Toast the bread and cut off the crusts if desired. Cut each slice of toast into four triangles.

4 Place the toast triangles on a baking tray and divide the cheese mixture among the triangles, pressing it down with the back of a teaspoon. Sprinkle with a little paprika and bake in the oven for 10 minutes. Serve hot or cold.

What do you think, Georgie, do they pass the test?

scallops baked
in white wine and garlic

Scallops will never be the same after I witnessed them being hand-caught on Loch Fyne. The shells were the size of side plates and the flesh like ice hockey pucks! Whilst filming Mitch and Matt's Big Fish, Chef Mitch Tonks and I carved them up straight from the water as they pulsed in our hands. These little gems taste so much nicer straight from the shell and it's a must to serve them in their natural environment; the sea air lingers and the punchy garlic butter magnifies the sweetness. Blink and the scallop will have dissolved in your mouth. Perfection!

SERVES 4   PREPARATION TIME 20 MINUTES   COOKING TIME 10 MINUTES

1 Preheat the oven to 230°C/450°F (gas mark 8). Using a fork, mash the butter, garlic, parsley and seasoning together in a small bowl.

2 Put two scallops in each half shell or two scallops in four individual ramekins on a baking tray if you can't get hold of the scallops in their shells. Add a splash of white wine and a scattering of salt to each shell or ramekin. Sprinkle over the tarragon and drizzle with olive oil.

3 Cover the scallops with the breadcrumbs and top with a knob of the garlic butter. Bake in the oven for 6 to 7 minutes, until the scallops are cooked and the breadcrumbs have formed a golden brown crust. Serve with lemon wedges.

75 g butter, softened
3 cloves of garlic, peeled and finely chopped
1 Tbsp finely chopped fresh parsley
Salt and freshly-ground black pepper
8 scallops (in the half shell if possible)
8 Tbsp dry white wine
1 Tbsp finely-chopped fresh tarragon
4 Tbsp olive oil
60 g breadcrumbs
Lemon wedges, to serve

Me, Mitch and our VW Combie! Although pretty to look at it just about survived the series... it broke down on the first day of filming!

mackerel kebabs

Any fishermen should take note of this beauty. Mackerel is one of the most, if not most underrated, British fish. Fried, barbecued or sashimi'd, it can either hold its own or other flavours brilliantly. Throw over the rod and wait only minutes for a mackerel's nibble, then one slash of the filleting knife later and it's ready! Skewer it up and fire up the disposable BBQ for a no-fuss meal in minutes.

SERVES 4   PREPARATION TIME 20 MINUTES   COOKING TIME 5 MINUTES

FOR THE TERIYAKI SAUCE

2 Tbsp soy sauce
2 Tbsp Chinese rice wine or pale dry sherry
1 tsp palm sugar
2-cm piece fresh root ginger, finely chopped
  (optional)
1 red chilli, seeded and finely chopped (optional)

FOR THE KEBABS

8 wooden skewers
2 mackerel, filleted, pin-boned and each
  cut into 4 equal pieces
4 spring onions, each cut into 4 pieces
Fresh mint and lime wedges, to serve

1 Soak the skewers in cold water for a couple of hours. This prevents them from burning during cooking. Preheat a barbecue or grill until very hot.

2 To make the teriyaki sauce, mix the soy sauce and rice wine with the sugar and stir to dissolve. If you want an extra kick, add grated ginger and red chilli to taste.

3 Place two skewers about 3 cm apart and skewer alternate pieces of fish and spring onion onto both at the same time. Repeat to make four double skewers in total.

4 Baste the skewers with the teriyaki sauce and put onto the barbecue or under the grill – the hotter, the better, as this will stop the fish sticking to the wire cooking rack. Continue to baste the fish with the sauce as it cooks. Cook for 3 to 5 minutes, turning once.

5 Serve the mackerel skewers with fresh mint and wedges of lime on the side.

carpaccio of salmon
with spring onion pancakes

I'm puffing my chest out because I'm a bit proud of this dish! It was my starter for the Celebrity MasterChef final. There's something quite fulfilling about creating a new dish you've never seen anywhere before. How a simple nut like me has an ambition to cook still baffles me, but the satisfaction of MasterChef judges John Torode and Greg Wallace applauding my creativity is something I didn't expect. Goodness knows what they would say about my book! I loved working with them both and without question they enabled me to express myself – thanks fellas! No turning back now.

SERVES 4 (MAKES ABOUT 12 PANCAKES)   **PREPARATION TIME 15 MINUTES**   **COOKING TIME 15–20 MINUTES**

1 Cover a baking tray with clingfilm. Arrange the salmon pieces in a single layer on the clingfilm. Cover with more clingfilm and bash with a rolling pin until they are as thin as smoked salmon. Chill until ready to serve.

2 To make the dressing, combine the crushed peppercorns, lime juice, oil and salt in a small jug and stir thoroughly.

3 To make the pancakes, sieve the flour and baking powder into a bowl. Season well and stir in the eggs and milk to form a thick batter. Purée half the spring onions and stir the puréed and chopped spring onions into the batter.

4 Heat a knob of butter in a non-stick frying pan and add four separate dessertspoons of the batter to the pan. Cook for 1 minute on each side, or until golden. Drain on kitchen paper and repeat until all the batter is used up, adding more butter if necessary.

5 To serve, place a quarter of the salmon in the centre of an individual serving plate, arrange three pancakes around the edge of the plate and drizzle the dressing over the salmon. Repeat to use the remaining pancakes and salmon. Sprinkle the cress over the salmon, to serve.

FOR THE SALMON AND DRESSING

300 g salmon fillet, skinned and cut into 4 equal pieces
1 tsp green peppercorns, crushed
Juice of 1 lime
4 Tbsp extra virgin olive oil
Pinch of Maldon sea salt

FOR THE PANCAKES

100 g plain flour
1 tsp baking powder
Salt and freshly-ground black pepper
2 free-range eggs, beaten
100 ml full-fat milk
4 spring onions, very finely chopped
Butter, for frying
Cress, to serve

figs with parma ham

What a conundrum! What to put on the menu for a dinner party... You don't want to spend all day in the kitchen but you still want your guests to feel that you've put in plenty of effort. The dressing lifts this cheeky little number into something more than just a piece of fruit and a slice of ham. Fresh, clean and zesty flavours set up the evening nicely. Plus you'd be surprised how many people have never tried figs but fall in love with them. All because of you!

SERVES 4   PREPARATION TIME 10 MINUTES

4 fresh figs at room temperature, stalks removed

4 slices of Parma ham, roughly torn

40 g wild rocket

1 Tbsp extra virgin olive oil

2 Tbsp balsamic vinegar

1 tsp clear honey

Salt and freshly-ground black pepper

1 Cut or break the figs in half and snake the torn ham around the figs in the centre of four small plates. Place the rocket leaves around the figs and ham.

2 Combine the olive oil, balsamic vinegar, honey and seasoning in a small cup and whisk well with a fork. Drizzle the dressing over the leaves just before serving.

light lunches and snacks

duck and melon salad

I wonder if my mum will ever try duck? She seems to have an aversion to it because, unlike chicken, you don't have to cook it all the way through; just a little pink is perfect. I am so desperate to make it appeal to her and I think the melon option might just work. Fruit and duck – the classic partnership. This dish reminds me of relaxing on the beach or being on holiday in Thailand, picking away at this delicious lunch. Come on Mum, join in!

SERVES 2   **PREPARATION TIME** 15 MINUTES   **COOKING TIME** 10–12 MINUTES

2 duck fillets (approx 225 g in total), skin on
Olive oil, for frying

FOR THE SALAD

50 g rocket
2 Tbsp unsalted cashew nuts
2 Tbsp chopped fresh coriander
2 spring onions, finely chopped
200 g melon in season, peeled, seeded and cut
   into 16 small slices (watermelon, Galia,
   Cantaloupe or honeydew can all be used)

FOR THE DRESSING

2 tsp sesame seeds
2 tsp toasted sesame oil
2 tsp soy sauce
2 Tbsp extra virgin olive oil
Zest and juice of 1 lemon

1 Preheat the oven to 180°C/350°F (gas mark 4). Heat a medium non-stick frying pan and fry the duck fillets on a high heat, skin-side down, for 2 minutes. Turn and cook for a further minute. Turn again and cook for 1 minute before transferring the fillets to a preheated roasting tin and place in the oven for 8 to 10 minutes.

2 Divide the rocket between two plates and sprinkle the cashew nuts, coriander and spring onions evenly over. Slice the duck fillet widthways into thin strips. Arrange the melon slices and duck fillet over the salad.

3 Combine the dressing ingredients in a small jug and stir well. Drizzle the dressing over the salad just before serving.

Me and Mum. She's the queen of traditional English food and an inspiration to me.

sweet and sour mussels

Here's a quirky alternative for mussels. This wonderful shellfish has the ability to absorb loads of flavour and of course the texture is unique. I first enjoyed these on a beach on holiday in Scotland, picking out the flesh from the shells with my fingers. The shells got tossed back into the sea and the bowl was licked clean.

SERVES 2   PREPARATION TIME 30 MINUTES   COOKING TIME 10 MINUTES

1 Discard any mussels that do not close when tapped. Put them in a large pan with the wine, cover and bring to the boil. Steam for 5 to 6 minutes, until the shells open. Drain and discard any shells that haven't opened. Set the cooked mussels to one side.

2 Heat the olive oil in the pan and add the chillies, garlic, spring onions and ginger. Fry for 1 to 2 minutes, then add the vinegar and sugar, and stir well.

3 Add the mussels and herbs to the pan and toss in the sauce. Serve hot with boiled rice and lime wedges.

1 kg live mussels, scrubbed, rinsed and beards removed
5 Tbsp dry white wine
1 Tbsp olive oil, for frying
4 red chillies, finely sliced
2 cloves of garlic, peeled and finely chopped
12 spring onions, chopped
2-cm piece fresh root ginger, peeled and finely sliced
150 ml white wine vinegar
1 Tbsp caster sugar
Small handful fresh basil (Thai if you can get it), roughly torn
Small handful fresh coriander, chopped
Boiled Thai rice, to serve
1 lime, quartered, to serve

In fact, why bother with rice and a plate? Why not share the bowl with your fellow diners?

light lunches and snacks

59

fritto misto

Britain is such a white fish nation. Cod, haddock and plaice top the bill, but there are numerous types of fish surrounding our isles that a vast majority of the public don't ever get to try. Believe me, you won't be disappointed when you lightly fry any fish in this style. This is a healthier alternative to battered cod, which can be heavy going. What's more, the taste of the fish, rather than the batter, is dominant.

SERVES 2   PREPARATION TIME 10 MINUTES   COOKING TIME 10–15 MINUTES

350 g mixed fish fillets, such as gurnard, mackerel, haddock or pollock, skinned and cut into strips

250 ml full-fat milk

3 Tbsp plain flour

Salt

Olive oil, for frying

Lemon wedges, to serve

1 Place the fish strips in a shallow dish and pour the milk over. Leave to soak for a couple of minutes.

2 Add a pinch of salt to the flour and place on a large plate. Take a piece of fish out of the milk and coat in the flour. Put the flour-coated strips on a clean plate and continue until all the fish is coated.

3 Pour olive oil to a depth of 1 cm into a large non-stick frying pan and heat to maximum heat. Place the fish a few pieces at a time into the oil to fry. Cook for 2 minutes on each side, then turn the fish over and cook for another 2 minutes. Remove with a slotted spoon and drain on kitchen paper. Repeat until all the fish is used up, and add more oil if necessary. Serve with lemon wedges on the side.

roasted vegetables
with salsa verde

There's no excuse: if the girls and boys at Merlin Elite Management can cook up this without any preparation, then anyone can do it! My good friend Richard Thompson asked me to teach the staff to cook as a team-building exercise. The memory of the day was Brea, my agent, somehow turning the salsa verde into mayonnaise. That'll be the oil and anchovy overload in the blender, Brea! Make sure you don't make the same mistake! Use seasonal veg as flavour is paramount and heightened by roasting.

SERVES 4   **PREPARATION TIME 25 MINUTES**   **COOKING TIME 40 MINUTES**

FOR THE ROASTED VEGETABLES

3 Tbsp olive oil
1 medium aubergine, roughly diced into
    2-cm cubes
1 large courgette, thickly sliced
1 bulb fennel, thickly sliced
1 red onion, peeled and thickly sliced
2 cloves of garlic, peeled and finely chopped
Sea salt and freshly-ground black pepper
1 whole red pepper
1 whole orange pepper
1 whole yellow pepper
4 sprigs fresh rosemary or 1 tsp dried rosemary
4 sprigs fresh thyme or 1 tsp dried thyme

FOR THE SALSA VERDE

20-g bunch fresh flat leaf parsley,
    thick stalks removed, roughly chopped
10-g bunch fresh basil, thick stalks removed,
    roughly chopped
10-g bunch fresh tarragon, thick stalks removed,
    roughly chopped
1 clove of garlic, peeled and finely chopped
1 Tbsp red wine vinegar
1 tsp Dijon mustard
1 anchovy fillet
½ Tbsp salted capers, rinsed
4 Tbsp extra virgin olive oil
Freshly-ground black pepper

1. Preheat the oven to 200°C/400°F (gas mark 6). Place the olive oil in a roasting tin and heat in the oven for 5 minutes. Add the aubergine, courgette, fennel, onion and garlic to the roasting tin, season, toss well and roast for 30 minutes, stirring occasionally.

2. At the same time, blacken the whole peppers in a separate tray in the oven or over a gas hob. Allow the peppers cool a little and then wrap each in clingfilm. When cooled, remove from the clingfilm and wash off the burnt skin. Cut into strips. Add the peppers and herbs to the roasting tin and stir well. Roast the vegetables for a further 10 minutes.

3. Meanwhile make the salsa, place all the ingredients, except the oil, in a food processor and whiz using the pulse action until you have a coarse paste.

4. Place the salsa in a medium serving bowl and gradually drizzle in the olive oil. Season to taste with black pepper and cover until ready to serve. Serve the vegetables with a good dollop of the salsa.

Watch and learn, Brea...

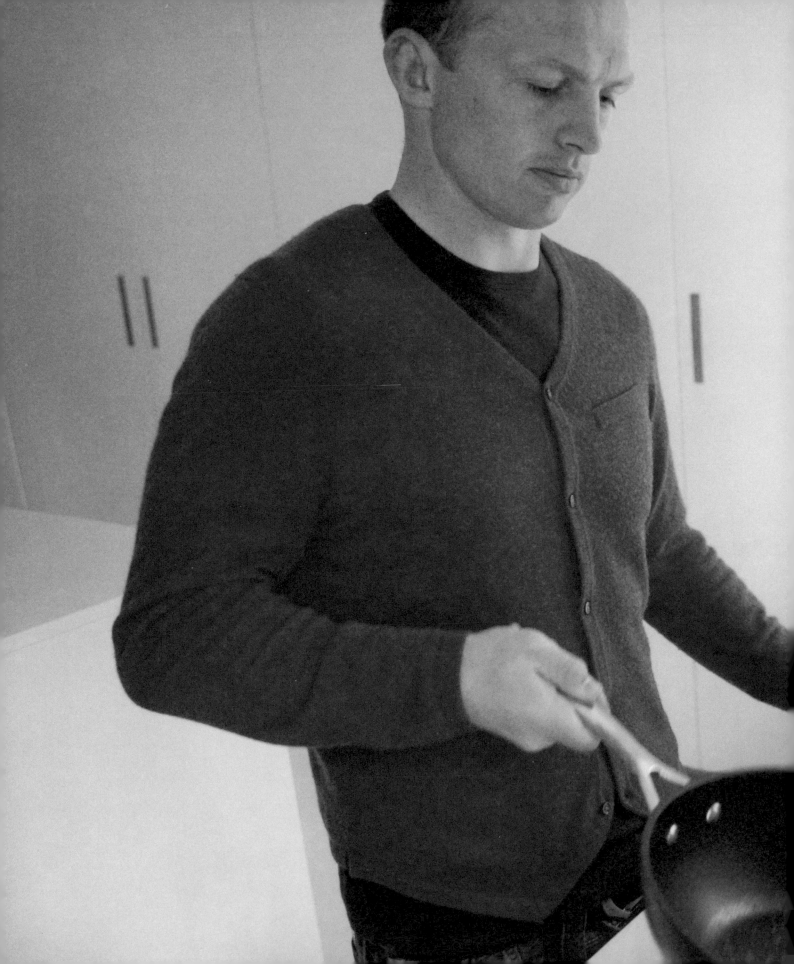

chicken teriyaki

We don't always have the best of summers, but how mental does the nation go when a warm evening draws in?! The green in front of my house fills up with picnickers and the smoke from next door's barbecue wafts over the fence. Yes, we all love a sausage or a burger thrown on, but if these bad-boy skewers get on the hot coals you'll have the local residents flocking. Never mind how good the chicken is, it's the chewy, charred edges that are nuggets of pure heaven!

SERVES 2   PREPARATION TIME 20 MINUTES PLUS AT LEAST 2 HOURS MARINATING   COOKING TIME 6–8 MINUTES

1 Combine all the ingredients for the marinade in a shallow dish and stir well. Place the chicken strips in the dish, season with black pepper and turn over a few times to coat thoroughly in the marinade. Cover and set aside in the fridge for at least 2 hours to marinate.

2 Meanwhile, place eight wooden skewers in cold water to soak for a couple of hours (this prevents them from burning during cooking).

3 Remove the chicken strips from the marinade and thread onto the soaked skewers. Barbecue on hot coals for 6 to 8 minutes or griddle instead (heat the olive oil to medium in a large griddle pan and cook the chicken skewers for the same amount of time, turning frequently until cooked through).

4 Serve the chicken skewers with salad and pitta bread.

FOR THE TERIYAKI MARINADE

1 Tbsp toasted sesame oil
2 Tbsp soy sauce
Juice of 1 lime
1 Tbsp clear honey
1 Tbsp whisky
2-cm piece fresh root ginger, peeled and finely chopped
2 cloves of garlic, peeled and finely chopped
2 spring onions, finely chopped
Freshly-ground black pepper

FOR THE CHICKEN

2 chicken breasts, each sliced lengthways into 4 strips
1 Tbsp olive oil
Salad and pitta bread, to serve

A little bit more chicken on the bone needed on my nephew Daniel.

houmous

Now that people are starting to realise that I love food, I get asked frequently to fill in love/hate questionnaires. Things like how did I get into food, what are my influences, my likes and dislikes and what do I snack on when I'm watching TV? Well, the answer to this last question is always the same – chopped carrots, cucumbers, pitta bread or nachos, and a tasty bowl of houmous. Am I weird?! I just love stuffing my face knowing that I can eat as much as I like and not worry too much about the consequences! OK, maybe a bit of garlic breath…

SERVES 2   PREPARATION TIME 10 MINUTES

1 Place the chickpeas, half the lemon juice, garlic, yoghurt, half the parsley and the seasoning in a food processor and whiz until smooth. Taste and add more lemon juice, salt and pepper if required.

2 Transfer the dip into a serving bowl, sprinkle the remaining parsley over and serve with the pitta bread and vegetable sticks.

400-g tin chickpeas, drained

Juice of 1 lemon

1 clove of garlic, peeled and chopped

3 Tbsp Greek yoghurt

2 Tbsp finely-chopped flat leaf parsley

Salt and freshly-ground black pepper

Warm pitta bread and raw vegetable sticks, to serve

salmon with coriander
and tarragon crème fraîche

Yes, the cooking time does say 2 minutes. No excuses there then. I'm a fish addict but sometimes simple takes over. Close your eyes and join me at my place in Arcos, Spain: a view of whitewashed Andalucían terraced houses, the thwack of the driver hitting balls onto the 12th fairway as I sip some fine Spanish sherry on the patio… I'm in paradise. All I need is this dish to dive into and then wipe away the crème fraîche from the corner of my mouth – mmm!

SERVES 2   PREPARATION TIME 5 MINUTES   COOKING TIME 2 MINUTES

10 g fresh coriander
15 g fresh tarragon
200 ml half-fat crème fraîche
Salt and freshly-ground black pepper
1 Tbsp olive oil
2 x 150-g salmon escalopes
Fine green beans or purple sprouting broccoli and tomatoes on the vine, to serve

1 Finely chop the coriander and half the tarragon leaves and stir them into the crème fraîche. Season well, cover and set aside.

2 Heat the olive oil in a large non-stick frying pan and cook the escalopes over a high heat for 1 minute on each side.

3 Serve the salmon hot or cold with the herby crème fraîche and either green beans, purple sprouting broccoli or tomatoes.

gazpacho

The first time I ever watched another of my heroes, Keith Floyd, on TV, he was on the Costa del Sol, surrounded by Brits abroad, attempting to make a bucket of gazpacho. He used no precise measures or quantities, but instead relied on his judgement: just fresh, raw ingredients thrown into a bucket (no sand) and whizzed up in an industrial blender. He did have a glass of sherry in the other hand, which may have accounted for his more casual style. But seriously, I love his passion and desire to make food accessible to everyone. I did get to meet him in Paris in 2007 and all that baloney about never meeting your heroes because you'll only be disappointed is rubbish. He was a total gent! I've used tinned tomatoes in this recipe: they are an easier alternative to removing the skins off fresh tomatoes and taste just as good.

SERVES 2   PREPARATION TIME 20 MINUTES PLUS 1 HOUR CHILLING

½ cucumber, peeled and finely chopped

½ red pepper, seeded and finely chopped

2 spring onions, peeled and finely chopped

Bunch of fresh basil

Bunch of flat leaf parsley

400-g tin plum tomatoes

1 stick of celery, finely sliced

2 cloves of garlic, peeled

1 red chilli, roughly chopped

4 Tbsp extra virgin olive oil

Juice of ½ lemon

Salt and freshly-ground black pepper

4 ice cubes, to serve

1 Reserve 1 teaspoon of each of the chopped cucumber, red pepper and spring onion, for the garnish, as well as a few basil and parsley leaves.

2 Combine the remaining cucumber, red pepper, spring onions and herbs with the tinned tomatoes, celery, garlic, chilli, olive oil and lemon juice in a food processor and blend until the soup is very smooth. Season to taste. Transfer to two soup bowls, cover with clingfilm and chill in the fridge for at least 1 hour before serving.

3 To serve, sprinkle the reserved chopped vegetables over the soup and garnish with the fresh herbs and plenty of freshly-ground black pepper. Add a couple of ice cubes to each dish and serve immediately.

peppered tuna salad

As I'm a food bore, I do this all the time: next time you're at a swanky restaurant and something takes your fancy, ask the waiter what's in the sauce/dressing. It can transform a dish into 5-star quality. When I went to Nobu in London I fell in love with their tuna sashimi salad to the point where I'd discreetly try to lick the plate clean. I only use five main ingredients in my dressing as they are readily available in the larder, but to my mates' naive palates they feel like they are back in the West End with chopsticks.

SERVES 2   PREPARATION TIME 10 MINUTES   COOKING TIME 1 MINUTE

1 To make the dressing, combine all the dressing ingredients in a small jug and whisk well.

2 Arrange the salad leaves in a small tower in the centre of two individual serving plates.

3 Press the crushed peppercorns onto both side of the tuna steak. Heat a non-stick frying pan over a high heat and quickly sear the tuna for no more than 20 seconds on each side.

4 Slice the peppered tuna and arrange the slices around the rim of the plate. Drizzle the dressing around the salad and serve immediately.

FOR THE DRESSING

5 Tbsp soy sauce
1 tsp sesame oil
1 heaped tsp Dijon mustard
2–3 shallots, peeled, rinsed and finely chopped
Freshly-ground black pepper

FOR THE SALAD AND TUNA

100 g of mizuna or baby leaf salad
1 Tbsp black peppercorns, crushed
250 g very fresh thick tuna steak

mini pizzas

Not only do I never fancy eating a whole 10-inch pizza, but by about the third slice I'm starting to get a little bored of the same taste. These little beauties are quick and easy to make (and eat!) and also give you the flexibility to try a few combinations of whatever tickles your taste buds. No more cardboard for lunch! They're full of fresh toppings your kids and mates will love.

MAKES 6   PREPARATION TIME 15 MINUTES   COOKING TIME 8 MINUTES

Butter, for greasing

35 x 22 cm sheet ready-rolled puff pastry

6 dessertspoons passata

1 tsp dried basil

3 slices of Parma ham, roughly torn

3 tsp pine nuts

6 dessertspoons grated mozzarella cheese

12 pitted black olives

Freshly-ground black pepper

1 egg, beaten

12 fresh basil leaves, to garnish

1 Preheat the oven to 220°C/425°F (gas mark 7). Lightly grease two baking trays.

2 Unroll the pastry sheet and using a 10-cm round cutter, saucer or plate, cut out six circles. Place the pastry circles onto the baking trays.

3 Spread the passata carefully over the circles, leaving a 1-cm border all around the edge. Top each pizza with a pinch of dried basil, some ham, pine nuts and mozzarella. Finally, put a couple of black olive in the centre of each pizza and season well with black pepper. Brush the pastry border with the beaten egg.

4 Bake the pizzas for 8 minutes, or until the edges have turned golden brown. Leave the pizzas on the tray to cool for a couple of minutes, remove with a fish slice, then top with a couple of basil leaves and serve warm.

tuna and rice noodle rolls

OK, let's slow it all down and allow cooking to become therapeutic. Chopping, slicing, rolling and finally eating. This is more of a technical dish, but it shows skills and patience your pals will really appreciate. Sushi is very fashionable at the moment, but preparing the rice is very time consuming so here's a speedy substitute. The guys at MasterChef weren't that impressed when I described this idea before the show. However, they ate their words – and all I had prepared afterwards. Cooking isn't all about ovens and hobs; flavours rule as far as I'm concerned!

MAKES 8 x 15-CM ROLLS   PREPARATION TIME 25 MINUTES

1 Combine all the ingredients for the dipping sauce in a small bowl. Set aside until ready to serve.

2 To make the pickled beansprouts, place the vinegar, a pinch of salt, two pinches of sugar and the beansprouts in a medium pan with 485 ml of cold water. Bring to the boil, then turn off the heat and allow to cool until ready to serve.

3 Place the noodles in a heatproof bowl and pour over enough boiling water to cover. Leave to stand for 5 minutes. Rinse the noodles thoroughly in cold water, then drain well.

4 Soften the first rice paper wrapper in warm water for 10 seconds. Remove the wrapper from the water and place on a flat surface. Place a little tuna, some strips of cucumber, carrot, spring onion and avocado, and a few noodles on one edge of the wrapper, then firmly roll it up. Repeat to use up all the mixture. It should make eight rolls.

5 Cut the rolls in half, arrange them on a serving plate on a bed of beansprouts and serve with the dipping sauce.

FOR THE DIPPING SAUCE

1 red chilli, seeded and finely chopped
3-cm piece fresh root ginger, finely grated
3 Tbsp palm sugar
Juice of 5 limes
1 clove of garlic, finely chopped
4 Tbsp Thai fish sauce
2 Tbsp cold water

FOR THE PICKLED BEANSPROUTS

150 ml rice wine vinegar
Salt and sugar, to season
50 g beansprouts

FOR THE ROLLS

40 g rice noodles
8 x 15-cm round Thai rice paper wrappers (banh trang)
150 g very fresh tuna or salmon steak, finely sliced
¼ cucumber, finely sliced lengthways
½ carrot, finely sliced lengthways
2 spring onions, finely sliced lengthways
½ avocado, finely sliced lengthways

my favourite cheese on toast

I know, I know, it's not cooking as such but cheese on toast is soooo good! When I was growing up, Sunday evenings were always the same: I'd finish my homework (in a rush), plead with my dad to watch Ski Sunday followed by Rugby Special. Mum would then bring in a bowl of homemade soup and three slices of the most perfect snack. The cheese has to cover every inch of the bread. Be generous with the topping because you'll love the string of melted cheese as it runs down your chin! The Tabasco sauce really spices up this simple snack but if you don't have any, just use chilli sauce instead.

SERVES 1   PREPARATION TIME 5 MINUTES   COOKING TIME 5–8 MINUTES

1 slice of thick white bread

1 tomato, finely sliced

Tabasco sauce, to taste

20 g Red Leicester cheese, finely sliced

Maldon sea salt and freshly-ground black pepper

1 Preheat the grill to high. Toast one side of the bread and flip it over. Place the tomato slices on the untoasted side of the bread and sprinkle over a few drops of Tabasco sauce. Place the sliced cheese on top and season well.

2 Return the bread to the grill and cook for 3 to 5 minutes, or until the cheese is bubbling and starts to brown.

Me with Mum and Dad on the Lions Tour in 2001 after the 3rd test in Sydney.

rice and pea salad

Here's one for all you active foodies. In order to maximise your training, eating at the right time of day is crucial. If this simple, tasty carb-loader is always handy it will make a huge difference. Plus I'm hoping the ingredients are those most people have in their cupboards – so you don't have to pop to the shops and put you off going to the gym!

SERVES 2   PREPARATION TIME 20 MINUTES   COOKING TIME 15 MINUTES

1   Make up the chicken stock in a measuring jug using the stock cube and 500 ml boiling water.

2   Grill the bacon for about 5 minutes, or until crispy. Meanwhile, heat the oil in a medium saucepan and fry the mushrooms for 2 to 3 minutes. Remove from the pan using a slotted spoon and drain on absorbent kitchen paper.

3   Add the onion and garlic to the oil in the pan and cook gently for 5 minutes. Add the rice, stock and plenty of seasoning to the pan. Bring to the boil, then reduce the heat, cover, and simmer for 5 minutes.

4   Add the cooked mushrooms, peas, sweetcorn and bacon to the rice and stir in.

5   Serve hot or cold. If serving cold, transfer the salad to a container and allow it to cool to room temperature. Once cooled, cover, refrigerate and eat within two days.

1 chicken stock cube

4 rashers back bacon, chopped into bite-size pieces

1 Tbsp olive oil

10 chestnut mushrooms, sliced

1 onion, peeled and finely chopped

1 clove of garlic, peeled and finely chopped

250 g long-grain white rice

Salt and freshly-ground black pepper

3 Tbsp frozen peas, thawed

100 g tinned sweetcorn kernels

FLORA
397
adidas

FLO

FIRST T

FLO

324

adi

steak salad

Picture the scenario: you're starving and you've just got home. It's getting late, maybe too late for a load of carbs. This juicy steak salad is just what you need. Now don't be scared of cooking the meat medium-rare as the juices mix with the dressing and complement the flavours. This is a fabulous throw-it-all-together meal and perfect for splashing and dribbling down your party frock. Napkins at the ready.

SERVES 2   **PREPARATION TIME** 20 MINUTES   **COOKING TIME** 6–15 MINUTES

2 Tbsp olive oil
3 cloves of garlic, unpeeled
Maldon sea salt and freshly-ground black pepper
4 Tbsp extra virgin olive oil
Juice of 1 lemon
2 large handfuls of salad leaves
10 cherry tomatoes, halved
6 spring onions, finely chopped
1 avocado, peeled and sliced
2 x 100–150 g sirloin steaks

1 Heat 1 tablespoon of the olive oil in a frying pan and fry the whole, unpeeled garlic cloves for 2 to 3 minutes. Remove from the pan with a slotted spoon and reserve the oil. Peel the garlic and place it in a mortar with $1/2$ teaspoon of sea salt, pound with a pestle to form a smooth paste.

2 Place the garlic paste in a small jug and stir in the extra virgin olive oil, the reserved garlic oil, the lemon juice and plenty of black pepper.

3 Arrange the salad leaves, tomatoes, spring onions and avocado slices on two plates.

4 Heat the remaining olive oil in the frying pan and pan fry the steaks according to your taste: for rare, cook the steak for 2 minutes on each side; for medium, cook it for 4 minutes on each side; and for well done, cook for 5 minutes on each side. Remove the steak from the pan and set aside, covered with foil, to rest for 5 minutes in a warm place.

5 Slice the steak into thin strips and arrange over the salad. Tip the steak juices into the dressing, stir well and pour the dressing over the steak and salad.

prawn linguine

Contrary to popular opinion, I'm not a show-off; I just love creating food for friends and family whenever they visit. I have even been known to travel with my own pots and pans! Harvey Thorneycroft was flabbergasted that I could rustle up this tasty dish off the cuff. Bless him – if only he knew just how simple it was. The bonus of cooking for Harvey is that he's the best business networker I know so now word is spreading fast that my prawn linguine takes some beating.

SERVES 2   PREPARATION TIME 10 MINUTES   COOKING TIME 10 MINUTES

250 g linguine

3 Tbsp olive oil

1–2 shallots, peeled and finely chopped

2 cloves of garlic, peeled and finely chopped

2-cm piece fresh root ginger, peeled and finely chopped

1 red chilli, finely chopped

8 raw king prawns, peeled

150 g frozen, peeled cooked prawns, defrosted

Maldon sea salt and freshly-ground black pepper

Chopped coriander or basil, to garnish

1 Cook the pasta according to the instructions on the pack.

2 Meanwhile, heat the oil in a large frying pan. Add the shallots, garlic, ginger and chilli, and cook over a medium heat for 30 seconds.

3 Add the king prawns to the pan and cook for 2 to 3 minutes, until they turn pink. Stir in the defrosted prawns to heat them thoroughly.

4 Drain the pasta and add to the frying pan. Stir well to coat the linguine with the prawn and chilli mixture. Season, garnish with the chopped coriander or basil and serve immediately.

Me with my great friend Harvey Thorneycroft after winning the second division title for Northampton Saints in 1996.

mains

halibut with anchovy butter

It's not all about frying, baking or steaming. How about poaching, and even more unique, poaching in olive oil? It sounds oily and a little over the top for such a fine fish but believe me it's legendary. I sat on a peninsula in Tarbet after having visited a halibut farm. Ahh... farmed fish, I hear you cry! Not in the slightest; these beautiful creatures were reared in enormous tanks of Loch Fyne water. They were handled magnificently and support the sustainable issue we all worry about.

SERVES 4   **PREPARATION TIME** 10 MINUTES   **COOKING TIME** 15 MINUTES

500 ml olive oil

3 cloves of garlic, peeled (2 left whole and 1 finely chopped)

4 x 150-g halibut fillets (sea bass, cod or haddock can be used instead)

1 Tbsp fennel seeds

150 g butter

6 anchovy fillets

2 Tbsp chopped flat leaf parsley

Juice of ½ lemon

½ tsp dried chilli flakes

Mash and steamed broccoli or green beans, to serve

1 Place the olive oil and the two whole cloves of garlic in a medium saucepan and heat on a low temperature. Add the fish and fennel seeds and cook gently for 6 to 7 minutes – the fish should poach and not fry. Spoon the oil over the fish a couple of times during cooking.

2 Meanwhile, in a small pan, gently melt the butter and add the remaining chopped garlic clove. Add the anchovies and allow them to melt into the butter. Add the parsley, lemon juice and chilli flakes, stir well and heat gently to warm through.

3 When the fish is cooked, remove it from the pan using a fish slice and drain on kitchen paper. Transfer to warmed plates, drizzle a little sauce over and serve the vegetables separately.

'rose and josh' curry

We've all got our signature dishes and when it comes to curry, each recipe is totally unique. When I was visiting my friends Kate and Justin Rose in Orlando, Florida, Justin was determined to prove that he could cook as well as he could swing a golf club. No skin off my nose as I was off on the driving range whilst he slaved over a hot stove. Anyway, his spin on rogan josh was amazing, with succulent meat, crunchy veg and a smooth, spiced sauce. Sickening that he's so good at everything. What made it worse, he thrashed me on the course the next day!

SERVES 6   PREPARATION TIME 25 MINUTES   COOKING TIME 1–1½ HOURS

1 Heat the oil in a large pan and gently fry 1 onion and half the mushrooms for 5 minutes. Stir in the garlic and spices, and fry gently for 2 to 3 minutes.

2 Add the lamb to the pan and fry until brown, for about 2 to 3 minutes, over a high heat, stirring constantly.

3 Add 150 ml water to the pan with the bay leaves, tomato purée and chopped tomatoes. Season, stir well, cover and simmer over a gentle heat for 30 minutes, stirring occasionally.

4 Stir in the second chopped onion, the remaining mushrooms, the finely chopped chilli and the coconut milk. Simmer for a further 30 minutes, stirring occasionally.

5 Remove the pan from the heat, stir in the spinach and cover. Leave for 5 minutes to allow the spinach to wilt. Stir well and serve with naan bread and rice.

2 large onions, peeled and finely chopped
250 g chestnut mushrooms, halved
3 cloves of garlic, peeled and finely chopped
1 tsp medium curry powder
½ tsp chilli powder
1 tsp paprika
½ tsp ground ginger
1 tsp ground cumin
700 g diced casserole lamb
2 fresh bay leaves
3 Tbsp tomato purée
400-g tin chopped tomatoes
Salt and freshly-ground black pepper
1 red chilli, finely chopped
150 ml coconut milk
180 g spinach
Naan bread and boiled basmati rice, to serve

At London's Ice Bar. One of J-Ro's curries would have gone down a treat here.

MEDIUM
CURRY POWDER

roasted vegetable lasagne

The staple diet of a rugby player, especially in the post-match function, consisted of two trays of carb-loaded grub. Curry, jacket potato, Shepherd's pie or even a fish supper. These dishes were always on rotation, but without fail lasagne would be the star choice. Garlic bread, Sir? Or maybe a side salad to go with the enormous dollop of overcooked rubbery effort of this Italian masterpiece. Not this recipe! Lasagne is traditionally served on its own, so leave it be. Bravo!

SERVES 6   PREPARATION TIME 55 MINUTES   COOKING TIME 3 HOURS

FOR THE TOMATO SAUCE

½ Tbsp olive oil
1 onion, peeled and finely chopped
4 cloves of garlic, peeled and finely chopped
1 green pepper, seeded and diced into 2-cm cubes
125 g mushrooms, sliced
1 tsp dried basil
1 tsp dried oregano
175 ml red wine
2 Tbsp tomato purée
2 x 400-g tins chopped tomatoes
Salt and freshly-ground black pepper

FOR THE ROASTED VEGETABLE FILLING

2 Tbsp olive oil
1 medium aubergine, diced into 3-cm chunks
2 medium courgettes, thickly sliced
1 red pepper, seeded and diced into 3-cm cubes
1 yellow pepper, seeded and diced into 3-cm cubes
1 bulb fennel, thickly sliced
1 tsp mixed dried herbs

1 Start by making the tomato sauce. Heat the oil in a large pan and fry the onion over a medium heat for 5 minutes. Add the garlic and green pepper, and cook for a couple of minutes. Stir in the mushrooms with the herbs, red wine, tomato purée and tinned tomatoes. Season well. Cover and simmer over a low heat for 2 hours, stirring occasionally.

2 Meanwhile, make the filling. Preheat the oven to 200°C/400°F (gas mark 6). Place the olive oil in a roasting tin and heat in the oven for 5 minutes.

3 Add the aubergine, courgettes, red and yellow peppers, and fennel to the roasting tin, season, sprinkle the dried herbs over and toss well. Roast for 40 minutes, stirring occasionally.

4 To make the cheese sauce, heat the butter in a medium pan and stir in the flour. Cook over a medium heat, stirring constantly, for a couple of minutes. Gradually add the milk and cook, stirring constantly until all the milk is added. Add the egg yolk and cheeses, and stir until the cheese has melted and the sauce has thickened. Season and add a pinch of cayenne pepper.

5 Preheat the oven to 180°C/350°F (gas mark 4). Grease a 25 x 35 x 6 cm ovenproof dish with the butter.

6 To assemble the lasagne, place half the pasta in the bottom of the dish, and top with half the tomato sauce and half the vegetables. Repeat the layering and top with the cheese sauce. Bake for 50 minutes or until golden brown and bubbling.

FOR THE CHEESE SAUCE AND PASTA

75 g butter
50 g plain flour
750 ml semi-skimmed milk
1 egg yolk
150 g mixed cheese (e.g. mozzarella, Cheddar, dolcelatte and Stilton), grated or finely chopped
Pinch of cayenne pepper
10 sheets dried lasagne
Butter, for greasing

pan-roasted chicken breasts
with caramelised butternut squash and green beans with shallots

When I was learning the fine art of cooking, Mark Edwards, the Group Executive Chef at Nobu, taught me how subtle changes in temperature, timing and seasoning could make a huge difference. He suggested I practise the same dish over and over so that my palate would improve. Pan-roasted chicken was the victim. Week after week I would try different ways of making it in my pursuit for perfection. I think I got there in the end. Hopefully you'll agree!

SERVES 4   PREPARATION TIME 30 MINUTES   COOKING TIME 30 MINUTES

5 Tbsp olive oil

900 g–1 kg butternut squash, peeled, seeded and chopped into wedges approximately 2 x 2 x 7 cm

2 Tbsp clear honey

Salt and freshly-ground black pepper

2 shallots, peeled and finely chopped

4 boned chicken breasts, with skin on

2 Tbsp finely chopped fresh rosemary leaves or 2 tsp dried rosemary

2 cloves of garlic, peeled and finely chopped

200 g fine green beans, topped and tailed

1 Preheat the oven to 200°C/400°F (gas mark 6). Place 2 tablespoons of olive oil in a roasting tin and heat in the oven for 5 minutes.

2 Add the butternut squash wedges to the roasting tin, drizzle with the honey, season well and place in the oven to roast for 20 minutes. Give the tin a good shake a couple of times during the cooking time to prevent the wedges from sticking.

3 Heat 1 tablespoon of olive oil in a large frying pan and gently fry the shallots for 2 to 3 minutes. Remove them from the pan and set aside.

4 Add the remaining 2 tablespoons of olive oil to the frying pan and brown the chicken breasts, skin-side down, over a medium heat for 1½ minutes. Place in a roasting tin, skin-side down, and sprinkle with the rosemary, garlic and plenty of seasoning. Turn the chicken a few times to coat evenly, finishing with it skin-side up.

5 When the butternut wedges have been roasting for 20 minutes, reduce the oven temperature to 180°C/350°F (gas mark 4). Place the chicken in the oven and roast the butternut squash and chicken for 10 to 12 minutes.

6 After the chicken has been cooking for 8 to 10 minutes, steam the beans over a pan of boiling water for 5 minutes. Stir the cooked shallots into the beans. Remove the wedges and chicken from the oven. Arrange the chicken breasts, green beans and a few butternut wedges on warmed serving plates and serve immediately.

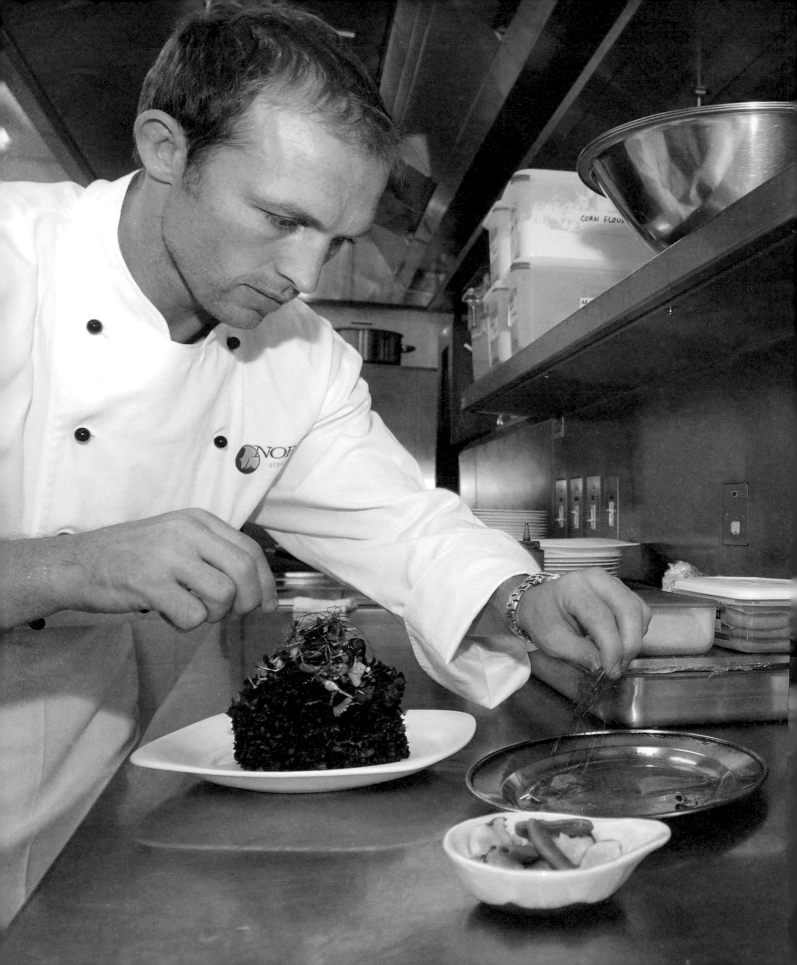

lamb chops
with chilli and rosemary

Because I love to get stuck into my food, the thought of chewing and sucking on the remains of a marinated lamb chop makes me salivate. Whether you cook this on the BBQ or under the grill, make sure the skin is crispy and the meat tender and pink. As an extra, add a few drops of truffle oil to the cabbage – now you're showing off.

SERVES 4   **PREPARATION TIME 10 MINUTES PLUS AT LEAST 1 HOUR MARINATING**   **COOKING TIME 15 MINUTES**

| 2 red chillies, finely chopped |
| 4 Tbsp finely-chopped fresh rosemary or 2 tsp dried rosemary |
| 1 clove of garlic, peeled and finely chopped |
| 4 Tbsp extra virgin olive oil |
| 8 lamb loin chops |
| Salt and freshly-ground black pepper |
| Mashed potatoes and steamed cabbage, to serve |

1 In a large shallow dish, combine the chillies, rosemary, garlic and oil. Place the chops in the dish, season well and turn over a few times to coat thoroughly in the marinade. Set aside for at least 1 hour to marinate.

2 Preheat the grill to high. Remove the chops from the marinade and place on the grill rack. Grill for 5 to 7 minutes on each side, until they are nicely browned but still a little pink in the middle. Transfer to a warm plate, cover with foil and allow the meat to rest for a few minutes.

3 Place two chops on each plate and serve with some mash and cabbage.

Do you reckon you could fit any more food on that barbie, Dad?!

traditional fish pie

Without doubt one of the nation's most popular meals. We've all got our favourite styles and methods but for me it's all about maintaining the texture and not creating a mush. Mitch Tonks insulted my mum's version on national TV but all said and done he taught me how to master the fish pie. It's not supposed to be fishy – more chunky and silky with a smooth sauce, plenty of seasoning, plus a crispy topping. Whack it in the middle of the table and let people help themselves and fight over the last scallop!

SERVES 4   PREPARATION TIME 40 MINUTES   COOKING TIME 30 MINUTES

800 g floury potatoes, peeled and chopped
120 g butter
1 leek, sliced
10 mussels, in their shells
100 g salmon fillet, skinned and cut into 3-cm chunks
100 g haddock fillet, skinned and cut into 3-cm chunks
100 g cod fillet, skinned and cut into 3-cm chunks
100 g smoked haddock fillet, skinned and cut into 3-cm chunks
4 scallops
450 ml full-fat milk
30 g plain flour
15 g roughly-chopped flat leaf parsley
100 g frozen, peeled, cooked prawns, defrosted
25 g Parmesan cheese, grated
Salt and freshly-ground black pepper

1 Bring a large pan of salted water to the boil and cook the potatoes until tender.

2 Meanwhile, heat 50 g of the butter in a small pan and gently fry the leek, stirring occasionally, until softened. Set aside.

3 Discard any mussels that do not close when tapped and remove the beards. Steam the mussels in a pan with 5 tablespoons of water for 5 to 6 minutes, until the shells open. Discard any that do not open. Remove the mussel flesh from their shells and set aside.

4 Put the salmon, haddock, cod and smoked haddock chunks into a large pan along with the scallops. Cover with 400 ml of the milk, bring to a simmer and poach for 2 minutes. Drain the fish and place in a heatproof serving dish, reserving the milk for the sauce.

5 Drain the cooked potatoes and mash with 20 g of the butter and the remaining milk. Preheat the oven to 180°C/350°F (gas mark 4).

6 Add the remaining 50 g of butter to the pan with the leek, heat gently to melt, and stir in the flour. Cook over a medium heat, stirring constantly, for a couple of minutes, then start to add the reserved poaching milk. Season and cook until thickened to the consistency of double cream. Remove from the heat and stir in most of the parsley.

7 Add the steamed mussels and prawns to the dish with the cooked fish and pour over the warm sauce.

8 Spread the mashed potato on top of the pie and sprinkle the Parmesan over.

9 Cook the pie for 15 to 20 minutes, or until the top is crisp and golden and the cheese has melted. Garnish with the remaining chopped parsley.

Mmm... I can't wait to tuck into Mitch's seafood spaghetti. There's nothing better than eating al fresco!

mushroom and asparagus
risotto

Carbohydrates are crucial to sports nutrition but they can lead to fairly tedious meals. Too much pasta and sauce, and rice and curry can get a little boring. But when an old friend called Brett Taylor made this for me, my outlook on eating carbs changed. When I make this dish at home, I have to calm myself down and not throw in too many varieties of vegetables all at once. This risotto is so creamy and tastes like it should be bad for you. Blimey, I live in the fast lane... Steady, Dawson!

SERVES 4   PREPARATION TIME 25 MINUTES   COOKING TIME 25 MINUTES

1 Preheat the oven to 200°C/400°F (gas mark 6). Gently heat the butter and olive oil in a medium flameproof casserole dish. Once the butter has melted, add the onion and garlic and cook gently for 5 minutes.

2 Add the mushrooms and rice to the dish and stir well to coat in the butter and oil. Pour the stock and wine into the dish and bring to the boil. Season and stir well. Remove from the hob, cover and place in the oven for 20 to 25 minutes, until the rice is tender, stirring a couple of times during cooking.

3 Meanwhile, steam the asparagus spears for 3 to 5 minutes, or until tender. Cut the asparagus into bite-size pieces.

4 Once the risotto is cooked, remove from the oven and stir in the cooked asparagus and the grated Parmesan cheese. Serve the risotto with plenty of freshly-ground black pepper and Parmesan shavings.

25 g butter
1 Tbsp olive oil
1 onion, peeled and finely chopped
2 cloves of garlic, finely chopped
300 g mixed mushrooms (e.g. chestnut, shiitake or oyster), roughly chopped
300 g risotto rice
700 ml good-quality vegetable or chicken stock
125 ml dry white wine
Salt and freshly-ground black pepper
125 g fine asparagus
40 g grated Parmesan cheese
Shaved Parmesan cheese, to serve

poached chilli chicken
with root vegetables

This is more of a mongrel dish. Is it a broth, is it a stew, or is it meat and two veg? I can't answer that because I don't really know the answer myself. However, after a chilly afternoon playing golf or a wet walk home from work, I can see you all curled up on the sofa devouring this dish. Great comfort food.

SERVES 4   **PREPARATION TIME** 20 MINUTES   **COOKING TIME** 20–25 MINUTES

2 medium carrots, peeled and cut into
   2-cm chunks

2 sticks of celery, cut into 2-cm chunks

500 g floury potatoes (e.g. King Edward or
   Maris Piper), peeled and cut into large chunks

1 onion, peeled

1 bay leaf

1 tsp dried chilli flakes

2-cm piece fresh root ginger, peeled and
   finely chopped

6 black peppercorns

Pinch of Maldon sea salt

15-g bunch of parsley

200 ml white wine

4 boned chicken breasts, with skin on

Chopped parsley, to garnish

1 Place the carrots, celery and potato chunks, whole onion, bay leaf, chilli flakes, ginger, peppercorns, salt, parsley and wine in a large pan.
Add enough cold water to just cover the vegetables and bring to the boil. Cover and simmer over a medium heat for 5 minutes.

2 Add the chicken breasts to the pan, making sure they are covered with the cooking liquid. Cover and simmer for a further 15 to 20 minutes, or until the chicken is cooked through. Remove the onion, bay leaf, peppercorns and parsley from the cooking liquid and discard.

3 Remove the chicken breasts from the pan, take the skin off and slice each breast into chunky pieces. Place each sliced chicken breast in the centre of an individual soup plate. Using a slotted spoon, remove the potatoes, carrots, and celery from the pan and divide equally between the plates. Pour over a little of the cooking liquid and sprinkle with parsley to garnish.

A corporate day out with my all-time hero, South African golf legend Gary Player (left).

turbot in parsley sauce

Turbot is an expensive favourite but it does bring out mixed emotions. It goes back to Vancouver in 1993 – myself and fellow rugby player Tim Rodber were both injured in a game and due to depart the tour so naturally we deserved a night out. Picture the scene: miserable and moody but sampling the delights of Canadian hospitality. Sitting under a canopy sipping a crisp Chablis and pondering over whether to go for the steak or the turbot. Only one winner there, then. It was the first time I had ever tried it and I will remember it forever. Soft, succulent and filling. Tim was gutted as he opted for the meat. Schoolboy error.

SERVES 4   PREPARATION TIME 20 MINUTES   COOKING TIME 5 MINUTES

2 Tbsp olive oil

4 turbot fillets (skin on), weighing about
  150–200 g each (sole or halibut can also be used)

25 g butter

25 g plain flour

300 ml semi-skimmed milk

Salt and freshly-ground black pepper

4 Tbsp chopped flat leaf parsley

Flat leaf parsley, to garnish

Boiled new potatoes and steamed green beans,
  to serve

1 Preheat the oven to 190°C/375°F (gas mark 5). Remove any small bones from the fish fillets.

2 Heat the olive oil over a high temperature in a large non-stick frying pan and sear the turbot fillets, skin-side down, for 30 seconds. Place the fish in a single layer, skin-side down, in a shallow ovenproof dish.

3 Melt the butter in a small non-stick pan. Add the flour and cook for 1 minute over a medium heat, stirring constantly with a wooden spoon. Gradually add the milk, stirring all the time. Season to taste and then stir in the chopped parsley.

4 Pour the hot sauce over the fish. Bake for 5 minutes or until the fish is opaque and flakes easily.

5 Using a fish slice, transfer each fillet to a plate, garnish with the fresh parsley and serve with minty new potatoes and buttered green beans.

langoustines thermidor

Thermidor… probably the most famous lobster treat. Naturally, the time of year determines the availability of lobster, so in order to appreciate the joys of a creamy tarragon sauce all year round, you can use langoustines instead. But if these prove difficult to get hold of or are too pricey, try king prawns – they're almost as good. This is top end cooking. Being able to rustle up this dish gives enormous satisfaction as for me Thermidor is a true classic.

SERVES 4   PREPARATION TIME 25 MINUTES   COOKING TIME 15–20 MINUTES

1 To prepare the langoustines, first remove the head using your fingers, then peel away the shell to leave the meat. Reserve the heads.

2 Pour the milk into a pan and add the onion, bay leaves and cloves. Bring to the boil, then simmer for a couple of minutes to infuse.

3 To make the sauce, melt half the butter in a medium non-stick pan and stir in the flour. Cook over a medium heat, stirring constantly, for a couple of minutes. Strain the infused milk and gradually add it to the flour and butter paste. Cook, stirring constantly with a wooden spoon, until all the milk is added. Stir in the mustard, cayenne and half the tarragon. Set aside.

4 In a large ovenproof frying pan melt the remaining butter, add the garlic and cook gently. Add the langoustine heads to the pan, squeezing them into the saucepan to get the juice out. Cook for 2 to 3 minutes to flavour the butter and then discard the langoustine heads, leaving the juices behind in the pan.

5 Preheat the grill to high. Add the peeled langoustines to the saucepan. Season well with black pepper and add the brandy or whisky. Boil for 1 to 2 minutes, then pour over the white sauce and gently warm through.

6 Sprinkle with the breadcrumbs and Parmesan, and place under the grill until the top is crisp. Garnish with the remaining tarragon and serve immediately with a green salad.

24 langoustines or 24 peeled raw king prawns
500 ml full-fat milk
1 onion, peeled and halved
2 bay leaves
6 cloves
50 g butter
3 Tbsp plain flour
½–1 tsp English mustard
Pinch of cayenne pepper
15-g bunch of fresh tarragon
2 cloves of garlic, peeled and crushed
Freshly-ground black pepper
Splash of brandy or whisky
20 g fresh breadcrumbs
20 g Parmesan cheese, grated
Green salad, to serve

venison burger

Not a common type of mince and you could of course use beef or lamb instead, but the slight gamey-ness of the flavour stands out enough to let you know it's not your standard burger. Venison was championed to me by a former rugby colleague, Tom Voyce. He's well into hunting, shooting and fishing. When he turned up with a lump of venison and told me to work my magic I was a bit stumped. Thankfully he likes a burger and eats like a horse, so enough said!

SERVES 4   PREPARATION TIME 15 MINUTES   COOKING TIME 8–10 MINUTES

2 Tbsp olive oil
1 small onion, peeled and finely chopped
1 clove of garlic, peeled and finely chopped
500 g minced venison
20 g fresh white breadcrumbs
1 egg, beaten
2 tsp Dijon mustard
1 tsp Worcestershire sauce
1 tsp tomato ketchup
Salt and freshly-ground black pepper
4 burger buns, salad leaves and cherry tomatoes, to serve

1 Heat 1 tablespoon of the olive oil in a large, non-stick frying pan and fry the onion and garlic over a medium to high heat for 2 to 3 minutes.

2 Transfer the onion and garlic to a large mixing bowl and add the venison mince, breadcrumbs, egg, mustard, Worcestershire sauce, ketchup and plenty of seasoning. Stir well with a fork to combine. Divide the mixture into four equal portions and with wet hands, shape the mixture into burger shapes.

3 Add the remaining tablespoon of oil to the frying pan and fry the burgers over a medium to high heat for 4 to 5 minutes on each side, or until cooked through.

4 Serve the burgers in the buns with the salad leaves and tomatoes.

Tom Voyce, nicknamed 'the horse', not because he eats like one but more because of his long face and blistering pace!

roasted rib of beef

Without question, a rib of beef is my favourite cut of meat. Slightly indulgent, but with the fat running through the beef it ends up so succulent. It's extremely suited to cooking in the Aga, but regardless of how or where you cook it, make sure you invest in a decent roasting tray to collect the juices ready for the tastiest gravy you've ever made. If you ever invite me over and serve this up don't accompany it with sprouts – I hate them! Maybe I should devise a recipe to convert myself...

SERVES 6   PREPARATION TIME 50 MINUTES   COOKING TIME 2–2¹/₂ HOURS

FOR THE BEEF

2.5-kg joint matured rib of beef on the bone
4 Tbsp plain flour
1 Tbsp mustard powder
Salt and freshly-ground black pepper

FOR THE RED CABBAGE

1 medium red cabbage, sliced
2 cooking apples, peeled, cored and roughly
   chopped
2 onions, peeled and roughly chopped
4 sprigs of fresh thyme
1 tsp ground nutmeg
3 Tbsp light brown sugar
3 Tbsp red wine vinegar
25 g butter, cubed

1 Preheat the oven to 220°C/425°F (gas mark 7).

2 Dust the joint all over with the flour, mustard powder and seasoning. Place in a roasting tin and cook at the top of the oven for 45 minutes. The meat should be well browned.

3 Meanwhile, prepare the red cabbage. In a large casserole dish place half the red cabbage, then half the apples and half the onions. Add the sprigs of thyme and sprinkle over half the nutmeg and sugar, season well. Repeat the layers and top with the remaining nutmeg and sugar, red wine vinegar and cubes of butter. Cover the casserole dish with a tight-fitting lid and set it aside.

4 Reduce the oven temperature to 180°C/350°F (gas mark 4) and cook the meat for 10 to 12 minutes per 500 g for rare meat, or 12 to 15 minutes per 500 g for medium rare.

5 Place the prepared red cabbage in the bottom of the oven and cook it for 1¹/₄ to 1³/₄ hours, stirring occasionally.

6 Half an hour before the meat is cooked through, prepare the parsnips. Place the olive oil in a roasting tin and heat in the oven for 5 minutes. Add the parsnips and roast them for 25 minutes.

7 Remove the joint from the oven, transfer to a plate and cover it with foil. Leave it to rest for at least 30 minutes.

8 Once the meat has been removed from the oven, increase the temperature to 220°C/425°F (gas mark 7) and roast the parsnips for a further 20 minutes.

9 To make the gravy, place the meat roasting tin over a medium heat on the hob and sprinkle in the flour. Cook, stirring constantly with a wooden spoon, for 2 minutes. Gradually add the red wine and then the stock, stirring all the time, until the desired consistency is reached. Pour the gravy into a serving jug.

10 Drizzle the honey over the parsnips and roast them for a final 10 minutes.

11 Heat the gravy in the microwave for 2 minutes. Carve the beef and serve it with the red cabbage, honey-roast parsnips, gravy and broccoli, or green vegetable of your choice.

FOR THE HONEY-ROAST PARSNIPS

4 Tbsp olive oil
4 parsnips, peeled and cut into 5-cm long chunks
2 Tbsp clear honey

FOR THE RED WINE GRAVY

2 Tbsp plain flour
150 ml red wine
400–500 ml beef stock

Steamed broccoli or your favourite green
   vegetable, to serve

roasted lemon poussin
with roasted new potatoes and rocket

If a full roast seems a little too heavy, this is the closest you'll get to a lighter version – perfect for those warmer days. There were a couple of pubs in the surrounding villages of Northampton that sometimes had this type of lunch on special. After a hard target battle at Franklin Gardens and a gallon of Guinness the night before, the usual suspects Grayson, Taylor, Rodber, Hunter and Thorneycroft would reconvene for late lunch and all dig in. Of course, the bird didn't last too long so more than one was needed. Oh yes, and plenty of spuds.

SERVES 4   PREPARATION TIME 15 MINUTES   COOKING TIME 55 MINUTES

4 poussins, each weighing about 500 g

4 lemons (2 quartered and 2 juiced)

25 g butter, melted

Maldon sea salt and freshly-ground black pepper

2 Tbsp olive oil

500 g baby new potatoes, or any larger potatoes, halved

4 Tbsp extra virgin olive oil

100 g rocket leaves

1 Preheat the oven to 190°C/375°F (gas mark 5). Place the poussins in a large roasting tin. Insert a couple of lemon quarters in each poussin. Mix the melted butter with the juice of one lemon, season well and brush the mixture generously all over the poussins.

2 Roast the poussins for 45 to 50 minutes, basting occasionally with the lemon butter.

3 Place the olive oil in a second roasting tin and heat it in the oven for 5 minutes. Add the potatoes to the roasting tin, season well and roast for 45 to 50 minutes, or until tender.

4 Check that the poussins are cooked by piercing the thickest part of the thigh with a skewer. When the juices run clear and there is no pink meat, they are cooked. Set aside, covered with foil, to rest for 10 minutes in a warm place before serving.

5 Combine the extra virgin olive oil with the remaining lemon juice and plenty of seasoning in a small jug. Add any cooking juices to the dressing, stir well and serve the dressing and roasted new potatoes separately. Place each poussin in the centre of an individual serving plate, surrounded by rocket leaves.

thai green curry

A relatively new addition to my repertoire. I've always loved Thai though. Thankfully, we have an awesome Thai restaurant on Chiswick High Road so I've drawn my inspiration from them. This dish is a massive favourite with sportsmen and women as it's low in fat and high in carbs. Plus, the magic of all the flavours tricks you into thinking you're eating something a bit naughty. And we all love that. Eating straight after or as near as possible to training is imperative to recharge the system. This has to compete with lasagne for the title of most frequently eaten dish in the post-match functions.

SERVES 4   PREPARATION TIME 25 MINUTES   COOKING TIME 20 MINUTES

FOR THE CURRY PASTE

5 medium green chillies, seeded and
   roughly chopped
2 lemongrass stalks, peeled, halved and
   lightly crushed
15 g fresh coriander leaves and stalks,
   roughly chopped
2 shallots, peeled and roughly chopped
2-cm piece fresh root ginger, peeled and
   roughly chopped
6–8 dried kaffir lime leaves, roughly torn
1 Tbsp ground coriander
1 tsp black peppercorns, crushed
1 tsp ground cumin
2 tsp soy sauce
3 Tbsp olive oil
Zest and juice of 1 lime
1 tsp Thai shrimp paste (blachan)

FOR THE CHICKEN AND VEGETABLES

1 Tbsp sunflower oil
4 chicken breasts, boned and skinned,
   diced into bite-size pieces
400 ml coconut milk
Juice of 1 lime
100 g fine green beans, topped and tailed
100 g baby corn, halved lengthways
100 g chestnut mushrooms, halved
Steamed jasmine rice, to serve

1 Place all the ingredients for the curry paste in a food processor or blender, add 2 tablespoons of water and blend to form a smooth paste.

2 For the chicken, heat the sunflower oil in a large non-stick frying pan and cook the diced chicken over a high heat for 5 minutes, or until it is just starting to brown. Use a slotted spoon to transfer the chicken to a plate.

3 Add the curry paste to the pan and cook it for 3 to 4 minutes over a medium heat. Return the chicken to the pan with the coconut milk, lime juice, green beans, corn and mushrooms. Cover and simmer for 10 minutes, or until the chicken is tender and cooked through, stirring occasionally.

4 Serve the curry on a generous bed of steamed jasmine rice.

grouse with crispy bacon
and port jus

All good things come to those who wait. And for only a few months in autumn, grouse is well and truly on the menu. It's a little pricey, so maybe save it for a special treat. I started my professional rugby career in Northampton, a town surrounded by sleepy, picturesque villages, rolling countryside and a thriving community. There's also plenty of game shooting going on there, so being the competitive spirit I am, I just had to join in. Unfortunately, there's no grouse in the Midlands but after an apprenticeship there I was invited up to Scotland by the Wilson family, who were avid supporters of Northampton RFC. No wonder these blighters are so lean: they dart about low and fast, making them almost impossible to shoot. I earned my supper eventually, well at least I think I did. But I have a feeling Giles Wilson took at shot at the same time as me. The jury's still out on that one...

SERVES 4   PREPARATION TIME 10 MINUTES   COOKING TIME 40–45 MINUTES

1. Preheat the oven to 190°C/375°F (gas mark 5). Place the birds in a lightly oiled roasting tin, season well, then drape the bacon slices over the breasts.

2. Roast for 35 to 40 minutes, until the juices run clear when a skewer is inserted into the thickest part of the thigh. Place the cooked grouse on a plate, cover with foil and allow to rest for 5 to 10 minutes.

3. Meanwhile, pour any cooking juices from the tin into a small pan, add the port and simmer gently for 5 minutes, stirring occasionally.

4. Serve the grouse with the port jus, mashed potatoes, carrots and cabbage.

4 oven-ready grouse
Olive oil, for greasing
Salt and freshly-ground black pepper
8 rashers streaky bacon
100 ml ruby port
Mashed potato, baby carrots and cabbage, to serve

mains

puddings

honey and raisin flapjacks

I'm not a tea or coffee drinker so I know I'm in the minority. However, I'd like to think I can still play host to friends and family when they pop over in the afternoon. I may not make the best brew but no one complains because they'll always pinch a couple of flapjacks from the jar. Don't be scared of experimenting with dried fruit: apricots, pineapple and prunes all work really well in this recipe – just replace the raisins with your favourite dried fruit or, if you're feeling particularly mischievous, mix two different types of fruit!

MAKES 10 BARS   **PREPARATION TIME** 20 MINUTES   **COOKING TIME** 40 MINUTES

110 g soft brown sugar

125 g butter, roughly cubed

1 dessertspoon clear honey

175 g oats

50 g raisins

1 Preheat the oven to 150°C/300°F (gas mark 2). Line a 20-cm square deep baking tin with greaseproof paper.

2 Place the sugar, butter and honey in a medium pan, and heat gently together until the butter has melted. Remove the pan from the heat and stir in the oats and raisins.

3 Spoon the mixture into the prepared tin and press it down evenly using the back of a metal spoon. Bake in the oven for 40 minutes.

4 Allow the mixture to cool in the tin for 20 minutes, then cut into bars. Leave in the tin until cold and then transfer to an airtight container for up to one week.

fresh pineapple wafers
with red chilli flakes

My mates must think I have far too much time on my hands to come up with 60 plus recipes for my first cook book. This idea came to me after eating strawberries with pepper at Wimbledon. Typically, I wanted a healthy option so instead of the cream, an LTA member suggested pepper. With that in mind and a lovely pineapple in the fridge, my thoughts turned to the spice drawer. Sticking out like a sore thumb was a jar of chilli flakes. Add a splash of lime juice and hey presto – go on Daws!

SERVES 4   PREPARATION TIME 10 MINUTES

1 medium fresh pineapple
Juice of 1 lime
Dried red chilli flakes, to season

1 To prepare the pineapple, remove the leafy crown with a sharp knife and slice a thin piece off the bottom. Slice the skin off the sides of the pineapple. Halve, then quarter the pineapple, then remove and discard the tough central core.

2 Slice the remaining fruit into very thin slices and arrange on a serving platter. Sprinkle the lime juice over and top with a few shakes of dried chilli (as if you were seasoning with black pepper). Use the chilli sparingly to start with and add more if you prefer a hotter flavour!

Looks like me and my sister have just been busted – but will they fall for the cheeky smile..?!

marbled blueberry
cheesecake

Thank goodness I don't have too much of a sweet tooth. Maybe that's why I enjoy cheesecake as it's not too sugary. Shoving a huge forkful into my mouth takes me back to when I was a kid and played mini rugby at Marlow RFC. After training, on a Sunday, Mum and Dad would take my sister Emma and me to the local pub for lunch. I couldn't be done quick enough with the main course. It was all about the cheesecake, scraping off the topping first and leaving the crispy biscuit base till last! Don't lie, I know you'll do the same when you tuck into this!

MAKES 23-CM CHEESECAKE   PREPARATION TIME 50 MINUTES PLUS 2 HOURS CHILLING TIME

1 To make the topping, place the blueberries and 50 g caster sugar in a small pan. Bring to the boil then reduce the heat and cook gently for 5 minutes, stirring occasionally. Allow to cool.

2 Grease and line a 23-cm round, deep springform tin. For the base, place the broken biscuits in a food processor and whiz to make fine crumbs. Alternatively, put the biscuits in a large food bag, twist the end closed and bash the biscuits with a rolling pin to form crumbs. Melt the butter in a medium pan over a low heat and stir in the biscuit crumbs. Press the mixture into the prepared tin with the back of a spoon to form a smooth base. Chill in the fridge while you continue to make the topping.

3 In a large mixing bowl, combine the cream cheese, remaining sugar and lemon zest. Stir well. In a small pan, gently warm the lemon juice, then remove from the heat. Squeeze the excess water from the soaked gelatine leaves and add them to the juice, stirring until dissolved. Allow to cool. Whisk the egg whites until they form stiff peaks.

4 Stir the lemon juice and gelatine mixture into the cream cheese mixture. Stir the double cream and then the soured cream into the mixture. Gradually fold the egg whites into the creamy mixture and pour the mixture over the prepared base.

5 Sieve the cooled blueberries and reserve the juice. Add spoonfuls of the cooked blueberries to the creamy topping and swirl through gently, using a metal spoon to create a pretty marbled effect. Carefully smooth the top and chill for at least 2 hours before serving. To serve, slice the cheesecake and serve on plates drizzled with a little of the reserved juice.

FOR THE TOPPING

225 g blueberries
150 g caster sugar
300 g full-fat cream cheese
Zest and juice of 1 lemon
5 sheets leaf gelatine, soaked in a bowl
  of cold water
2 egg whites
150 ml double cream
150 ml sour cream

FOR THE BASE

Butter, for greasing
300 g digestive biscuits, broken
150 g unsalted butter

apricot and cinnamon
bread and butter pudding

Friday nights, before every England match, grown men of enormous strength and power would run through the hotel at dinner time like school children. Bread and butter and sticky toffee puddings were the treats of the week. Dave Reddin, our fitness director, was in charge of supplying both on the menu, hoping to put us in a good frame of mind for the following day's match. Simple things impress simple souls. Maybe that was England's secret to World Cup victory in 2003, the mighty 'B&B'.

SERVES 6   PREPARATION TIME 20 MINUTES   COOKING TIME 25–30 MINUTES

1 Preheat the oven to 180°C/350°F (gas mark 4). Lightly grease a 28 x 20 x 5 cm ovenproof dish with butter.

2 Spread the softened butter over the bread and cut each slice into four triangles. Layer the bread and apricots in the dish.

3 In a large jug combine the milk, eggs, sugar, nutmeg and cinnamon. Pour the mixture over the bread and apricot mixture. Press the bread into the liquid with the back of a metal spoon.

4 Bake for 25 to 30 minutes, or until golden. Serve the pudding hot with cream, custard or cinnamon ice cream.

Butter, for greasing
30 g butter, softened
6 thick slices white bread
100 g ready-to-eat dried apricots, finely chopped
550 ml semi-skimmed milk
3 free-range eggs
30 g soft brown sugar
Generous grating of fresh nutmeg
1 tsp ground cinnamon
Cream, custard or Cinnamon ice cream (see page 152), to serve

frozen berries
with hot vanilla and white chocolate sauce

Girls, this doesn't get any better. I know you're all total chocoholics so join me in total heaven. All in moderation ladies (and gents), so go easy on the number of times you make this a week! Balance is vital, so maybe load up on the berries. Watch the piping hot chocolate give off just enough heat to thaw the berries. I defy anyone not to dive straight back in for more. One mouthful just isn't enough.

SERVES 4   PREPARATION TIME 5 MINUTES   COOKING TIME 5–10 MINUTES

100 ml single cream

1 vanilla pod

100 g white chocolate, broken into pieces

300 g frozen mixed berries (e.g. blackberries, raspberries, blackcurrants and redcurrants)

1 Pour the cream into a small non-stick pan. Place the whole vanilla pod in the cream and gently heat.

2 In the meantime, melt the chocolate pieces in a heatproof bowl over a pan of simmering water, making sure the bottom of the bowl isn't touching the water. When the chocolate has melted and the cream is warm, remove the vanilla pod from the pan (rinse and dry it and it can be used again) and stir the cream into the chocolate.

3 Arrange the berries on four individual serving glasses. Pour the warm sauce over the berries.

frangipane tarts

Let me set the scene – the final of MasterChef. All the pressure is on the delivery. I'd officially screwed up my lemon tart in the quarter final so it was time to make amends. I love a challenge and it was just as well after I realised I'd leant on the on/off oven switch whilst blind baking my pastry. Whoops! After a bit of flapping about and preciously watching the clock, the tart came out a real delight. (All that fuss over a tart!)

MAKES 6 TARTS   PREPARATION TIME 45 MINUTES PLUS 30 MINUTES CHILLING TIME   COOKING TIME 25–35 MINUTES

1 Grease 6 x 11-cm loose-bottomed flan tins. To make the pastry, sift the flour into a large bowl. Using both hands, rub the butter into the flour until it resembles fine breadcrumbs. Stir in the sugar.

2 Stir the egg yolks into the mixture using a table knife, until the dough begins to stick together in lumps. Add 1 to 2 tablespoons of water if the mixture seems too dry.

3 Bring the dough together with one hand and knead it very lightly for a few seconds to give a smooth, firm dough. Wrap the dough in clingfilm and leave it to rest in the fridge for 30 minutes.

4 Meanwhile, prepare the filling. Combine the almonds, butter, sugar, flour and eggs in a medium bowl and beat well, using an electric whisk, until creamy and smooth.

5 Preheat the oven to 180°C/350°F (gas mark 4). Cut the dough into six equal pieces. Dust a work surface with flour and roll each piece out to a circle large enough to line the flan tin – don't forget the sides!

6 Line each tin with a pastry circle and lightly press the pastry into the flutes. Carefully trim the edges of the case with a knife to remove any excess pastry and prick the pastry with a fork. Place the tins on two baking sheets and bake for 10 to 15 minutes.

7 Divide the filling between the tins. Slice the pear halves, fan out and arrange on top of each tart. Bake for 15 to 20 minutes, or until the filling is set and a light golden brown.

8 Carefully remove the tarts from the tins, dust with icing sugar and serve with cinnamon ice cream or crème fraîche.

FOR THE PASTRY

Butter, for greasing
200 g plain flour
100 g butter, cubed
100 g caster sugar
3 egg yolks

FOR THE FILLING

75 g ground almonds
75 g butter, softened
75 g soft, light brown sugar
50 g self-raising flour
2 eggs, beaten
3 ripe pears, halved, peeled and cored
Icing sugar, to dust
Cinnamon ice cream (see p 152) or crème fraîche, to serve

rice pudding

A favourite of my sister's, Emma. If I'm honest, I'm not a big fan of the skin on rice pudding whereas when we were kids she virtually climbed across the table to hog it all. 'Not so fast Emma', my Dad would say, as he was also partial to the crispy, chewy rice pudding topping. My mum would just raise her eyebrows and tut. Emma would offer to do the washing up if she could have a spoonful more than Dad. Happy memories. For a bit of zing, add a little lemon zest before serving.

SERVES 4   PREPARATION TIME 10 MINUTES   COOKING TIME 1½ HOURS

Butter, for greasing
100 g short-grain pudding rice
50 g light soft brown sugar
700 ml semi-skimmed milk
1 whole nutmeg

1 Preheat the oven to 150°C/300°F (gas mark 2). Grease a 1.5-litre ovenproof dish.

2 Place the rice in a sieve and rinse it well under cold running water. Drain thoroughly then pour it into the prepared dish.

3 Stir in the sugar and milk. Grate plenty of nutmeg over the top of the pudding.

4 Cook for 30 minutes then stir thoroughly. Return to the oven for 1 hour, or until it is thick and creamy with a golden brown skin.

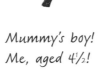

Mummy's boy! Me, aged 4½!

fruit salad

Not the most creative of recipes, I admit, but this is purely advisory. I'm always popping in and out of the house – meetings, golf, TV, radio, hooking up with friends or just going for a run. I am very rarely around the house for more than a few hours. so having an enormous bowl of fresh fruit available ticks so many boxes for me. Throw it in the blender for a smoothie, use as a topping for pancakes or add a big dollop of yoghurt to it. Maybe add to your favourite cereal too. It's so versatile and it just takes a measly 15 minutes of chopping and preparing. If you keep it in a sealed box it will keep for up to four days.

SERVES 4   PREPARATION TIME 15 MINUTES

1 Place all the fruit and the lemon juice in a large serving dish. Stir carefully to combine and chill until ready to serve. Serve with a large dollop of yoghurt.

220-g tin pineapple chunks in juice
1 apple, cored and chopped into bite-size chunks
1 pear, cored and chopped into bite-size chunks
2 kiwi fruit, peeled and sliced
10 strawberries, hulled and halved
4 Tbsp blueberries
½ cantaloupe or Galia melon, peeled, seeded and chopped into bite-size chunks
Juice of ½ lemon
0% fat Greek or plain low-fat yoghurt, to serve

Me after a tough round of golf with Scotland rugby captain Gavin Hastings (far right) and golfer Miguel Angel Jimenez (centre right).

mrs dawson's
carrot and orange cake

Thanks to my mum I rarely forget to phone my grandparents on their birthday. They'll all be laughing at me as I'm notorious in the Dawson/Thompson family for my memory deficiency. Mum also knows that I don't eat a lot of sweet things but a fruit or carrot cake doesn't last long in my cupboard. I finally bribed her for her secret recipe so that the Dawson legacy may continue from generation to generation. Let's hope that one day I have children who cook!

MAKES 20-CM SQUARE CAKE   **PREPARATION TIME** 40 MINUTES   **COOKING TIME** 35–40 MINUTES

1 Preheat the oven to 180°C/350°F (gas mark 4). Grease and line a 20-cm square deep baking tin.

2 Combine the sugar, eggs and oil in a large mixing bowl and stir well with a wooden spoon. Add the raisins, orange zest and grated carrots, and stir. Sift the spices, flour and bicarbonate of soda into the bowl, and stir thoroughly until all the ingredients are incorporated.

3 Pour the mixture into the tin (it will be quite runny) and bake for 35 to 40 minutes, until it is springy when pressed in the middle. Allow the cake to cool in the tin for 10 minutes. Turn the cake out of the tin onto a wire rack and remove the paper.

4 Once the cake is completely cool make the icing. Sieve the icing sugar into a medium bowl and mix in the orange juice, stirring well until smooth. Drizzle the icing over the cake using the back of a metal spoon to spread it out evenly, and sprinkle the orange zest on top to decorate.

FOR THE CAKE

Butter, for greasing
180 g light brown sugar
3 eggs
180 ml sunflower oil
80 g raisins
Zest of 1 large orange
3 medium carrots, peeled and grated
Generous grating of fresh nutmeg
1 tsp ground cinnamon
180 g self-raising flour
1 tsp bicarbonate of soda

FOR THE ORANGE ICING

180 g icing sugar
2–3 Tbsp orange juice
Zest of 1 orange

chocolate mousse pots

Everyone's been asking me what desserts I'm going to feature in this book because they know I don't have a sweet tooth. That is true but now and again dinner just isn't dinner without a little chocolate hit! Not too rich or sweet but light and lip-lickingly good! When you serve it up, tell your kids you're not happy with it because it smells a bit funny – as they go in for a sniff, dunk their nose in the chocolate goo! My nephew Daniel falls for it every time!

SERVES 4   PREPARATION TIME 25 MINUTES PLUS 2 HOURS CHILLING TIME

150 g 70% cocoa solids dark chocolate, broken into small pieces

3 large free-range eggs, separated

4 whole hazelnuts and grated white chocolate, to decorate

1 Place the chocolate pieces in a large heatproof bowl over a pan of simmering water, making sure the bottom of the bowl isn't touching the water. Stir the chocolate occasionally with a wooden spoon and when it has all melted, stir well and remove the bowl from the pan.

2 Beat the egg yolks into the warm chocolate and stir well (it will go quite thick at this stage).

3 Whisk the egg whites in a clean bowl until they form stiff peaks. Fold the egg whites carefully into the chocolate, two tablespoons a time, using a metal spoon.

4 Divide the mousse between four small white mugs, place a hazelnut in the centre and sprinkle the white chocolate over. Chill for a couple of hours before serving.

cinnamon ice cream

No question this is a winning dish. When I was fighting it out in the Celebrity MasterChef final I knew this pud would knock the judges' socks off. Not the sweetest of ice creams but full of spice and flavour – a great accompaniment to the Frangipane tarts on page 145 or a simple bowl of fruit. I love the look on a guest's face when you present a tub of homemade ice cream at the end of a BBQ.

SERVES 6   PREPARATION TIME 30 MINUTES PLUS 6 HOURS FREEZING

50 g caster sugar
2 cinnamon sticks
250 g mascarpone cheese
500 ml ready-made custard
2 tsp ground cinnamon
100 ml double cream

1 Place 100 ml water, the caster sugar and cinnamon sticks in a small pan. Heat gently, stirring constantly until the sugar dissolves. Remove from the heat and allow to cool for 20 minutes.

2 Meanwhile, place the mascarpone in a large mixing bowl and stir well with a fork to soften. Carefully stir the custard and ground cinnamon into the softened cheese. Fold in the double cream using a large metal spoon.

3 Remove the cinnamon sticks from the cooled syrup. Gradually add the syrup to the mascarpone, beating well with a fork between each addition. If using an ice cream maker, continue following the manufacturer's instructions. Alternatively pour the mixture into a freezerproof container with an airtight lid. Cover with the lid and freeze for 2 hours.

4 Remove the ice cream from the freezer and beat well to break up the ice crystals. Re-freeze for a further 2 hours and then repeat the process. Return to the freezer until completely frozen. To serve, remove the ice cream from the freezer 20 minutes before serving and place in the fridge to soften.

VARIATIONS

Tutti frutti ice cream
Make as above but omit the cinnamon sticks in Step 1. Add 150 g finely-chopped mixed dried fruit, such as apples, peaches, pears, apricots, prunes, pineapple, mango, cherries, melon or papaya to the sugar syrup once you have taken the pan off the heat. In Step 2 omit the ground cinnamon.

Pistachio ice cream
Make as above but omit the cinnamon sticks in Step 1. Replace the ground cinnamon in Step 2 with 100 g finely-ground pistachio nuts. Stir the pistachio nuts into the mixture at the end of Step 2, before the sugar syrup is added.

apple and walnut
crunch crumble

Touring with rugby teams was some of the most fun I've ever had, travelling to all corners of the globe to test yourself against some of the greatest players. Whether it was with England or the British and Irish Lions, part of the experience was sampling the local food. South African braai, a type of roasted meat, New Zealand hungi, and some of the biggest steaks I've ever seen in Argentina – you name it, I've eaten it – but none of it compares to your own creature comforts. So Clive Woodward decided to take our very own chef with us wherever we went. All of a sudden our favourite dishes were rustled up on request; no more moping around for weeks on end yearning for fish and chips or a decent lasagne. For me it was about tucking into a piping hot apple crumble – don't forget the custard!

SERVES 6   PREPARATION TIME 30 MINUTES   COOKING TIME 35–40 MINUTES

1 Preheat the oven to 190°C/375°F (gas mark 5). Place the apples, sugar and cinnamon in a medium pan with 2 tablespoons of cold water. Bring to the boil, then reduce the temperature and cook over a low heat, stirring occasionally, until the apples are just beginning to soften; this should take about 10 minutes. Place the cooked apples in a 1.5-litre ovenproof dish.

2 To make the topping, place the two types of flour in a mixing bowl and rub the butter into the flour using your fingertips until the mixture resembles breadcrumbs. Stir in the sugar and walnuts.

3 Spoon the crumble mixture evenly over the apples and bake for 35 to 40 minutes. Serve piping hot with cream or custard.

FOR THE APPLES

1 kg cooking apples, peeled, cored and quartered
20 g soft brown sugar
1 tsp ground cinnamon

FOR THE TOPPING

80 g wholewheat flour
80 g plain flour
80 g unsalted butter, cubed
120 g soft brown sugar
80 g walnuts, roughly chopped
Cream or custard, to serve

index

picture credits

Matt Dawson: pages 35, 56, 67, 84, 97, 107, 132, 146, 147, 156.

Getty Images: pages 86–7, 114–15, 140–41, 157.

Martin Lovatt: page 90.

Gary Moyes: pages 32, 47, 109, 123.

Nobu Group: pages 78, 104.

Luca Zampedri: page 7.